WALKING
— THE —
EMPOWERMENT
TIGHTROPE

WALKING
— THE —
EMPOWERMENT
TIGHTROPE

BALANCING
MANAGEMENT
AUTHORITY
&
EMPLOYEE
INFLUENCE

ROBERT P. CROSBY

KING OF PRUSSIA, PA

Prepared for publication by Organization Design and Development, Inc. Printed in the United States of America.

Library of Congress Catalog Card Number: 92-60828
ISBN: 0-925652-15-6

This book is for the manager who has been searching for practical ideas about how to create stellar performance. It is for the manager who is ready to act.

Contents

Preface xi

Acknowledgements.. xiii

Cycle Toward Creating and Maintaining a High Performance Team xv

Chapter One: Empowerment and High Performance 1

    The Future Organization 6
    What Follows in This Book 7

Chapter Two: The 25 High Performance Factors 9

    Step One: Appraise Your Group..................................... 9
    Step Two: Review the Results 16
    Step Three: Develop an Improvement Plan 18
    Step Four: Involve Your Employees in Analysis,
                Problem Solving, and Follow-Through..................... 19

Chapter Three: Action Ideas for the 25 Factors 20

    1. Obtain Clear Sponsorship 21
    2. Be Open 23
    3. Build Influence Structures. 26
    4. Be Clear about Your Decision-Making Style 28
    5. Make Decisions 31
    6. Implement Those Decisions 32
    7. Identify Input 34
    8. Create Effective Throughput 35
    9. Get Feedback on Output. 38
    10. Improve Meetings 42
    11. Build a Climate for Creativity 45
    12. Clarify Roles/Jobs 47

13. Make Sure There Is a Person/Task Fit 48

14. Clarify Authority 50

15. Make Sure That Resources Are Available 51

16. Develop Team Measurements. 53

17. Paint the Big Picture 59

18. Provide for Relevant Just-In-Time Training 61

19. Set Priorities 63

20. Clarify By-Whens 64

21. Commit to Follow-Through 64

22. Identify Single-Point Accountability 67

23. Reinforce Success 68

24. Reprimand Poor Performance 70

25. Constantly Maintain Good Work Relationships..................... 72

Chapter Four: Focus on System Change, Not Individual Change ... 75

The Powerful But Forgotten Performance Formula 76

We All Interpret Differently 81

The Most Difficult of All Human Skills 82

The Limitations of Training 83

Skewing the Equation the Other Way 84

Distinguishing Between the Approaches 87

Role Confusion: A Typical Systems Issue 92

Chapter Five: Survey Feedback — Turning Data Into Action ... 95

What Does Work? 95

Doing Survey Feedback with Your Employees 96

Dimensions of the Survey Feedback Process and Action Steps 97

How Does Turning Data Into Action Work in a Large System?...... 99

Observations 101

The Staircase Model for Large Organizations 101

Appendices

Appendix A   Self-Managing Teams

Appendix B   Three States of Group and Organizational Systems

Appendix C   Role Clarity — Example: Quality Engineering Organization

Appendix D   Macro Performance Indicators

Appendix E   High Performance Indicators — Short Form

Appendix F   An Example of One Industry's Adaptation of the 25 Factors to Fit Its Values and Needs

Appendix G   Specificity Quiz

Appendix H   Brainstorming Rules

Appendix I   Action Recommendations/Commitments

Appendix J   Characteristics of an Effective Facilitator

Appendix K   Orientation Session

Appendix L   Data Feedback and Problem-Solving Session

Appendix M   Follow-up Meetings

Appendix N   An Exercise in Distinguishing Between Openness and Personal Confession

Appendix O   The Interpersonal Gap by John L. Wallen

Appendix P   Managing Meetings of Matrixed Task Forces/Committees for Results

Appendix Q   The OD (Organizational Development) Practitioner as Organizer — Proactive Consulting

Appendix R   Graphic Illustration of the Change Process

Preface

Without clear authority, no one is empowered — not the manager, staff, or hourlies — no one. And, all need to be empowered — appropriately! The paradox is that everyone already has power. Industrial sabotage, apathy, and the failure to identify quality issues are unproductive uses of power. So empowerment is really about helping people to channel the power they already have toward qualitative and productive ends. The positive relationship between empowered people and productivity/quality is surely clear to the reader. What often is not clear is that empowerment is for everybody. If the hourlies are not clear about power or using their power appropriately, then the CEO and supervisors of each unit also are not effectively using their power. Intuitively knowing this, bosses work the extremes — they are either too tough or too lax. This book is for the boss who would manage from the middle — that is, balance management authority with employee authority. It encourages decisiveness, clarity about who decides what, and the appropriate sharing of influence.

A major problem in organizations is the exercise of either too much management authority and power, or the other extreme — abdication. *Empowerment programs are falsely aimed at hourlies* and as such are doomed to go the way of other fads and slogans. *Authority must be balanced.* There is a degree of authority and influence that is appropriate to everyone in an organization. Clarity about the appropriate balance is our theme. The practical application of that theme permeates the how-to action ideas that form the heart of this book. Do not think of this book as *yet another program* but as a process intended for managers of a single unit or larger group who will start managing differently.

Robert P. Crosby
Seattle, Washington
July, 1992

Acknowledgments

First, a special thanks to my colleague and wife, Patricia. She helped me so much in editing, writing, and *doing* this book that sometimes I say "our" book. While the theory is mine, her touch appears on nearly every page.

Thanks to Terry Schmidt for three years of dialogue in the early formulation of this book in the mid-80s.

Executives who were clients and who contributed to my learning in the 1980s were:

> David Theilman, E. Z. Loader Boat Trailers; Ross Smith, Carnation; Joe Firlit, formerly with the Sacramento Municipal Utility District; and Corbin McNeil, Philadelphia Electric.

They'll find familiar stories in this book. So will John Ward of Management Analysis Company, who was both an employer and client extraordinaire.

When I write the word "sponsor" — an important one in this book — I think of these leaders and especially another executive at Philadelphia Electric, David Helwig. Thanks David for creating a space where both personal and organizational change could actually happen. Also at Philadelphia Electric, thanks to Rob Schachter (a graduate of the Leadership Institute of Seattle — LIOS) for carrying high the torch of excellent organizational consultation.

And thanks to executive Don Simonic and internal consultant Tom McCombs (a LIOS grad) at Alcoa for riding with Patricia and me on an exciting organizational journey. Also, at Alcoa there were the nine hourly workers who were amazing change agents:

> Ray Bowles, Dennis Christianson, Ken Dahlke, Ed Grimm, Ron Hanson, Ed Hatcher, Jr., George Kelch, Mark Lindman, and Vicki West.

Cycle Toward Creating and Maintaining a High Performance Team

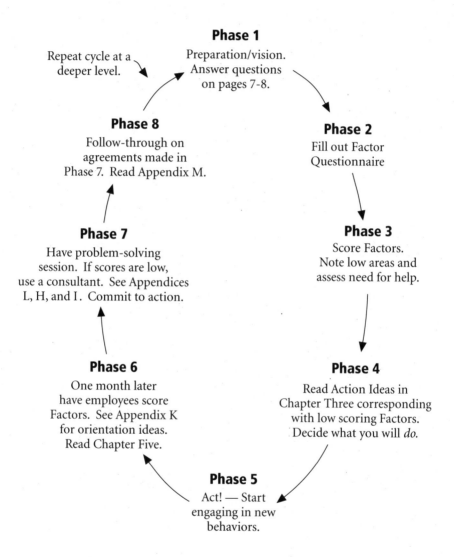

Phase 1
Preparation/vision.
Answer questions
on pages 7-8.

Repeat cycle at a
deeper level.

Phase 8
Follow-through on
agreements made in
Phase 7. Read Appendix M.

Phase 2
Fill out Factor
Questionnaire

Phase 7
Have problem-solving
session. If scores are low,
use a consultant. See Appendices
L, H, and I. Commit to action.

Phase 3
Score Factors.
Note low areas and
assess need for help.

Phase 6
One month later
have employees score
Factors. See Appendix K
for orientation ideas.
Read Chapter Five.

Phase 4
Read Action Ideas in
Chapter Three corresponding
with low scoring Factors.
Decide what you will *do*.

Phase 5
Act! — Start
engaging in new
behaviors.

Chapter One

Empowerment and High Performance

The struggle between decisiveness and influence is an ongoing dance. That leaders and followers need each other is surely in the category of a universally accepted axiom. Equally obvious is the tragedy perpetuated in the 20th century from dysfunctional dances when the balance was missing. Usually there was too much authority placed in the *leader,* or too little. This has been true in nations, organizations, and families. The familiar polarization in families between the over-authoritarian parent and the permissive parent is also manifest in large systems. More accurately, authorities often are inconsistent and flip from being authoritarian to being permissive and back again. The statement about parenting, "Parents are authoritarian until they can't stand themselves and then permissive until they can't stand the kids,"[1] also characterizes much management behavior.

Finding the appropriate balance in leadership style is extremely difficult. This book has been written for the manager who is ready to do a different dance but not give up the leadership role that is appropriate and desperately needed. "The goal is to change the organizational *dance* in such a way that the whole system experiences change . . . and . . . if you change your individual *dance,* the whole system will react."[2]

---

[1] The author associates this statement with the Parent Effectiveness Training work of Thomas Gordon. He published a book with that same title.

[2] From training materials written by Ron Short of The Leadership Group, Seattle, WA.

The creation of an empowered and high-performing organization is dependent on several factors. The author, using his personal experience and data from over 500 United States, Canadian, and British organizations, has identified 25 factors that impact performance.[3] When these factors are attended to, productivity and quality are high, absenteeism is low, accidents are reduced, and employees are more likely both to enjoy and be motivated in their work environment. In other words, people are empowered.

The good news is that these factors are influenced primarily by the manager of a work team. While individual motivation is important, the dominant force in a work team is the line manager.[4] Managers are not elected, but there are important parallels between political democracy and democracy in the work place. For instance, the role of leadership cannot be abdicated. There is no democracy without authority. The art of managing is to balance the imagined polarities between authority and influence.

The jargon *self-managing teams* (autonomous work teams/self-directed teams) is popular today. (See Appendix A for more about self-managing teams.) Unfortunately, many employees and managers define such teams without taking into account the need for clear management authority. It is our experience that teams will fail without the balance we describe. The tension in political democracy between freedom and justice, and between citizen influence and government authority, will be with us forever. Likewise, the struggle in organizations about how to tap the energy and expertise of employees, while also managing with optimum authority, is an ongoing one.

This struggle cannot be solved by the extremes of authoritarianism or permissiveness. Further, management by consensus as the exclusive style,

---

[3] Data is from the *People Performance Profile* (PPP),™ Computer Profiles, Inc., Narberth, PA. These key factors were presented by Robert Crosby in 1986, at a NASA conference on Productivity/Quality. The original PPP was developed in 1979 by Robert Crosby and John Scherer (Spokane, WA), assisted by Dr. Ron Short (Seattle, WA).

[4] The reference is to those in management with legitimate authority. This may be the foreperson or unit supervisor.

rather than only when appropriate, is a disaster. When overused, consensus is time consuming and is often controlled by the most rigid or resistant members. (This will be further developed in the Action Idea for Factor 4, page 28.)

Toward understanding the desired balance, little attention has been given to two factors that were crucial to the Japanese success story. First, the Japanese had a long history of authority that was rooted in the family. After the Great War, when they developed effective ways to involve workers, they did so in the context of accepted authority. Employee influence was not translated to mean the abdication of authority by management.

Our Canadian and US consulting experiences have been otherwise. Both managers and employees often have unrealistic and dysfunctional expectations about the minimized role of authority when terms like participative management, employee involvement, or self-managing teams are used. Either the employees think they will be deciding everything or, at the other extreme, that the new emphasis is really the old authoritarianism in a new mask. Usually management is equally confused.

The word democracy is paradoxically suspect among US and Canadian managers. It is a politically prized term, but it is often equated with permissiveness or lack of leadership in the business sphere.

Also, when we read in the New York Times about the Volvo Uddevalla humanistic manufacturing experiment in Sweden, we wondered if the same lack of clear leadership and authority may not have been an important variable. It takes 50 hours of labor to build a car at Uddevalla. In contrast, the time required to build a car in Japan is 17 hours and in the United States, 25 hours. The Uddevalla plant workers take longer to assemble a car than the workers at the other three more traditional Volvo plants. "The approach, which entailed slashing layers of management and eliminating all foremen . . . (also aimed to) give them (the employees) more control over their jobs."[5] I would rather have retrained the foremen and groups to achieve the balance emphasized in this book.

---

[5] *New York Times*, July 7, 1991, Business Section, p. 5.

A second factor that may have influenced Japanese success is the apparently deeply imbedded cultural belief described by Joseph Campbell as follows:[6]

> The Buddhist teaching . . . the *Doctrine of Mutual Arising* . . . implies that no one — nobody and no thing — is to blame for anything that ever occurs, because all is mutually arising. That fundamentally is one reason why in Japan, even shortly following World War II, I found among the people I met no resentment. Enemies mutually arise: they are two parts of the one thing. A leader and his following also are parts of the one thing. You and your enemies, you and your friends: all parts of the one thing, one wreath: "thing and thing: no division."

This context is not easy to come by in the United States. Managers must strive constantly to recreate a nonblaming work context. The productive context is one of making it work rather than finding fault and blame. Without this frame or way of seeing, authority will be viewed as existing primarily for punishment (of the blamed) rather than for vision, support, and clarity. Messengers will continue to get *shot*.

Context is powerful. How you think and speak about employee influence is highly instrumental in your creation of the work culture. Ideally, employee influence applies to every employee, from the least paid to the CEO. It is a process of fully utilizing the talents and experiences of everyone.

Top managers depend on an effectively functioning middle and bottom. More than any others, middle managers work in a void. Top managers often wonder what it takes to get things operating the way they want. *The basic context is that employee influence truly means that all employees, from the hourly to the CEO, be empowered.*

---

[6] Joseph Campbell, *Myths to Live By*, Bantam Books, New York, 1973, p. 148.

Also, as stated above, empowerment must be implemented in the context of *making it work*. In the context of finding fault, griping, and blaming, employee influence and involvement is a negative, defeating force. *Making it work* means that anything can be discussed with minimal defensiveness. Finding fault means that underlying causes will be avoided, people will be defensive, feedback will be distorted, and empowerment efforts will fail. Finding fault focuses on the narrow spectrum of what is wrong. *Making it work* encourages a search for new opportunities for productivity and facing up to persistent problems. The fundamental basis for effective influence is a shift in this context. The action ideas in Chapter Three can help you achieve this shift.

Another crucial context is *economics*. Employee influence is about economic success. Companies have to make money; competition is tough. Employees know that today, more than ever, they have seen many companies fail. Empowerment done well increases productivity. That it also creates a better and more humane work place is a happy corollary. The economic context is believable. *With* that context clearly acknowledged, company leaders are more believable when they discuss employee influence. *Without* that context being central and visible, people tend to disbelieve organizational leaders. Employee influence communicated as a patronizing, do-good activity is doomed.

Leadership demands truth and clarity. Emphasizing empowerment for both hourly employees and management will appear contradictory to many. Entering the 20th century, management models were authoritarian. The use of authority entering the 21st century will be influenced by the events of the past 100 years. The contribution of the labor movement in the early part of this century was an essential corrective step. Of course, the pendulum has swung sometimes and tyranny has come from the opposite direction — from labor. Pendulum swings seem inevitable.

Perhaps a functional use of authority cannot emerge until after a history of the old authoritarianism, followed by a needed rebellion against that tyranny, with labor union successes and excesses, and then extreme permissive kinds of management styles where nobody knew who was in charge or who was making the decisions.

Without experiencing the above, it is difficult to understand a goal-oriented, humanistic leader who gives people influence *and* recognizes that it is *absolutely essential to give authority to someone for certain functions in order to "make it work."* (See Factor 4.) Our history had to be what it was in order for management and labor, in this new balance, to empower each other and give up the destructive, adversarial relationship.

The Future Organization

The organization of the future *must* achieve the balance we are describing here. The leader must wield strong enough authority to create a participative culture, which paradoxically creates a loyalty that enables followers to march toward organizational objectives in a way unimagined by the "old school" authoritarian bosses.

I was part of a volunteer organization in which medical doctors and other people with high social status followed the lead of a 22-year old who said, "Okay, to get this room ready for this activity, we need the wastepaper baskets emptied." And they would do it because they wanted to make it work. They were not there to fulfill their status needs but out of a concern for the larger mission of that particular organization. An empowered organization breaks through the bureaucracy of status and encourages initiative from whomever sees what needs to be done.

The opportunity to do productive work in a humane organization, with clarity of direction, is a privilege denied to many. And it is the most powerful motivating and self-esteem enhancing force known. It also leads to bottom-line results. However, a differentiated leader with such clarity is rare. Throughout this book I will refer to the difference between a differentiated and an undifferentiated leader. It is difficult to comprehend an organization with clarity and without a differentiated leader.[7] Before moving to Chapter Two, I recommend that you read the reference in Appendix B defining these terms.

---

[7] See Appendix B for a definition and graphics of differentiation — *Three States of Group and Organizational Systems.*

What Follows in This Book

Chapter Two consists of a simple, self-scoring instrument that identifies the 25 key Factors that impact performance. Also, I have outlined four basic steps for a manager to take to help the work team improve its performance.

Chapter Three is a how-to manual. There I illustrate with action ideas how successful managers have balanced their authority with employee influence in the 25 key areas. The leaders' clarity about the context that they intend to create is of paramount importance. Of course, external factors also impact success. The economic scene, national work ethic, distribution of wealth and privileges, and market position of the product being produced are critical. Also, a manager with about 10 employees in a small business certainly is more influential than one in a large organization where his/her group is one of many. Depending on the situation, the manager may have varying degrees of influence with his/her employees. But whatever your internal or external situation, we invite you to create a top-flight organization. The ideas in Chapter Three could help you do that.

Because I believe that survey feedback is a powerful tool for affecting change, I have included instructions in Chapter Five for using the instrument in Chapter Two as a survey feedback tool. Two versions of the instrument are included. The longer version is more descriptive of the Factors. Also, I have included a chapter, *Focus on System Change, Not Individual Change,* that illustrates fundamental concepts upon which this book is based.

To set the stage for what comes next, answer the following questions:

1. What is the mission of your group? If you are part of a larger organization, what is the organization's stated mission? What is your "piece of the larger pie"?

2. What are the values that are important to you? Are your organizational values dynamic and referred to constantly, or are these values simply slogans that are not influencing day-to-day activities? If the latter, what are your real values?

3. What are your business objectives? What do you want to achieve in the next 12 months?

4. Who supports and has ownership of all of the above? You? Your boss? Your people?

5. Are the mission, values, and business objectives known and integrated with the daily work life? Do employees know what they can do to impact these? Do they know their "piece of the pie"?

6. Are organizational progress reports regularly made available to all employees?

7. Are you able to state your *specific* business objectives and values for your unit, and clearly specify what you expect from your employees to help achieve these? (See *Specificity Quiz,* Appendix G.)

How you answer these questions will impact the successful use of this book. Activities suggested will be of minimal use if done randomly and without your own emerging clarity about your intentions.

When you are reasonably clear about your objectives and are ready to involve employees appropriately, then you may create a strategy to achieve high performance with your team/crew. The 25 High Performance Factors and activities will give you ideas for your strategy, but strategy is driven by the clarity you have about your objectives.

Chapter Two

The 25 High Performance Factors

Have some fun as you appraise your work group along the 25 Factors listed below. As noted in the introduction, these Factors were developed through extensive research and experience. Building an improvement plan from these Factors will upgrade your group's performance. There are four steps you will need to follow. Take the first three steps now and the final step a month from now.

Step One: Appraise Your Group

Step One is to fill out the following inventory. For each item, circle the number on the continuum that best represents your work group.

High Performance Factors

1. Sponsorship

The supervisor firmly supports his/her direct reports providing direction, resources, clarity, and enthusiasm to guarantee success.

Almost Always   Almost Never

| 5 | 4 | 3 | 2 | 1 |

2. Openness

Data flows accurately so that problems are identified. Disagreements are viewed as opportunities for dialogue and are dealt with directly.

Almost Always   Almost Never

5	4	3	2	1

3. Influence

Employees have input and influence on factors that impact their work life, i.e., suggesting solutions, often seeing suggestions being acted on, and getting feedback when suggestions are rejected.

Almost Always   Almost Never

5	4	3	2	1

4. Distinguish Between Decision Making and Influence

Managers are clear about the distinction between "who is deciding" versus "who is influencing" and communicate that.

Almost Always   Almost Never

5	4	3	2	1

5. Decisions Are Made

Decisions are made in an expedient amount of time; it does not take forever to get a decision made.

Almost Always   Almost Never

5	4	3	2	1

6. Implementation

Once decisions are made they are effectively implemented in a timely way.

Almost Always   Almost Never

5	4	3	2	1

7. Input Needs

We get on time and with quality what we need from outside or inside suppliers, such as materials, maintenance support, information, equipment, and/or commitments to service.

Almost Always   Almost Never

5	4	3	2	1

8. Throughput

Once input is received, we are organized in the best possible way to produce quality output in a timely manner with clear and efficient processes. Our equipment is up-to-date and effectively used.

Almost Always   Almost Never

5	4	3	2	1

9. Output

We give to others what they need and provide excellent service, on time and with quality. This includes internal customers (within this organization) or external customers.

Almost Always   Almost Never

5	4	3	2	1

10. Meetings

Our meetings are effective. Time is not wasted. Appropriate people attend. Participation is shared. When needed, we solve issues and decisions are made.

Almost Always   Almost Never

5	4	3	2	1

11. Creativity

New ideas for improving work processes, communication, product development, etc., are encouraged. It is easy in our climate to suggest or try something new.

Almost Always   Almost Never

5	4	3	2	1

12. Job Clarity

I know exactly what I am to do. My boss' expectations are clear. My job does not unnecessarily duplicate someone else's job.

Almost Always   Almost Never

5	4	3	2	1

13. Person-Task Fit

The right people are doing the right tasks. My skills and the skills of others are being used effectively here.

Almost Always   Almost Never

5	4	3	2	1

14. Authority

People have the authority to do what they are expected to do. They typically do not have to be persuaded or manipulated to act in the absence of higher authority.

Almost Always   Almost Never

_____

5   4   3   2   1

15. Resource Availability

We are able to get the resources we need to do our job well. These include information, equipment, materials, and maintenance.

Almost Always   Almost Never

_____

5   4   3   2   1

16. Team Measurements

We have measurements that help us regularly track key factors related to our input, throughput, and output so that we can monitor and quickly solve identified problems and issues.

Almost Always   Almost Never

_____

5   4   3   2   1

17.   Big-Picture Perspective

We know the larger picture, i.e., where our organization is headed, how world and national economic and competitive factors affect us, and how we are doing. On everyday tasks we know why we are doing what we are doing.

Almost Always   Almost Never

| 5 | 4 | 3 | 2 | 1 |

18.   Training

Members of our work team are well-trained technically as well as in teamwork and communication skills.

Almost Always   Almost Never

| 5 | 4 | 3 | 2 | 1 |

19.   Priorities

No time is wasted wondering which task is more important. Priorities are consistently clear.

Almost Always   Almost Never

| 5 | 4 | 3 | 2 | 1 |

20.   By-whens

Whenever a decision is made, someone clarifies who will do what and by when. Also, by-whens are not only *given* to bosses but *received* from them as well.

Almost Always   Almost Never

| 5 | 4 | 3 | 2 | 1 |

21. Follow-Through

Commitments are effectively tracked, i.e., reviewed at subsequent meetings or tracked by computer. Missed commitments are discussed and recommitted or are reassigned to someone else.

Almost Always   Almost Never

5	4	3	2	1

22. Single-Point Accountability

There is one person accountable for each task. Even on a matrixed group across departments, one person holds the single-point accountability rather than the group.

Almost Always   Almost Never

5	4	3	2	1

23. Reinforcement

People are appreciated for work well done. Expressions of thanks are clear enough so that the receivers know precisely what they did that was liked.

Almost Always   Almost Never

5	4	3	2	1

24. Reprimands

When our supervisor is unhappy with our work, he/she tells us as soon as possible, privately. The reprimand is clear and very specific about the unappreciated work or action but not accusatory, judgmental, or vindictive.

Almost Always   Almost Never

5	4	3	2	1

25. Work Relationships

Work relationships are maintained. When two or more people disagree, the issue is dealt with directly and effectively rather than avoided or escalated.

Almost Always   Almost Never

5	4	3	2	1

Step Two: Review the Results

Now add up the scores you gave to the 25 Factors. Here are some guidelines for evaluating your score.[8]

107 and Above — Outstanding

Congratulations, your group is among the rare, high-performing groups we have studied. Chances are that you most likely are an open, non-defensive, problem-solving manager who balances caring of your employees

---

[8] The author has a large base of data from the *People Performance Profile* results. Guidelines suggested here are derived from that data and do not reflect a large base of scores from these self-scored factors.

with clarity about expectations. Of course, your employees may see it differently. We usually find that managers score higher on these items than do employees. In a month, if you follow our plan, you will find out if this is true in your case.

95 to 106 — Excellent

Your group is in the top tenth of those we have studied (extrapolating from the PPP). You are doing very well and could easily reach a higher goal.

77 to 94 — Good

Many work groups score in this range. Applying the tips that follow can easily boost your scores. Achieving a higher level of performance is within reach.

76 and Under

The majority of groups score here. Opportunities abound. We commend you on your honesty. To make improvements you may need some coaching from someone else in the company or from an outside consultant. The lower your score the greater the need for you to seek skilled, outside help.

A skilled consultant sees patterns. That is, he/she sees these 25 dimensions happening or not happening. Of course, agreeing or intending to do things differently is not the same as actually doing so. A skilled consultant notices when intentions (be they ever so noble) do not match the patterns or ways of behaving within the organization or group.[9] In a how-to manual such as this one, it is easy to be seduced into thinking that following certain steps can produce predicted results. But it does not always work that way; some behaviors are deeply ingrained. For example, the triangulation referenced in Activity 25 (Work Relationships) is a pattern developed in the family and

---

[9] See *The Interpersonal Gap*, by John Wallen, Appendix O.

carried into the work place. Openness (2), Decision and Influence patterns (3, 4, and 5), Creativity (11), Authority (14), Follow-Through (21), Reinforcement (23), and Reprimands (24) are examples of other High-Performance Factors that may not change simply as a result of implementing the processes suggested. A skilled consultant will see these dysfunctional patterns and do (not just say) something to help you shift toward a more effective style.[10]

Also, you may want to consult with two or three other managers who have scored these Factors. Share your scores and support each other by suggesting tips in areas where each of you has high scores. Others may also have opinions about your patterns of interaction.

Step Three: Develop an Improvement Plan

Review the items where scores were lower than you wish and think about some specific ways to improve them. Examples of what other managers have done follow in Chapter 3. Use the examples to stimulate your thinking as you develop a one-month improvement plan, which you then implement prior to the next step.

At this stage, you are *not* starting a program. We suggest that you do not announce anything. Rather, *by your behaviors,* declare your intent to make things better. People despair of words, words, words. They look for action. So, rather than talking about it, do it! Dance differently. Create!

How Do I Create?

By your actions! By your language![11]

You are your words, your actions, and your language. If your words are: Probably; Hopefully; If I can; I'll try; I don't know when; It wasn't my

---

[10] See Appendix Q for an article about consulting.

[11] Robert Crosby has written similar words in his values book, *Living with Purpose When the Gods Are Gone,* Times Change Press, Ojai, CA, 1991.

fault; Nobody told me . . . then you will create a high percentage of not achieving, of blaming, and of finding excuses. Essentially (your essence), you will face the world as an excuse and an avoider.

If your words are: Here's what I expect; How can I support you?; When do you need this from me?; I'll complete it by (when); Here's when I need this from you; What difficulties does that present to you?; I'll handle that; . . . then you will create a high percentage of achieving. Essentially, you will face the world as one whose *word is truth.*

You create a new context by your words. When you look an employee in the eye and say, "I'll make sure you have that answer by Wednesday noon," you will have begun the transformation. It begins with you!

If an item is on the employee's front burner but on your back burner, then you may request from that employee a reminder the day before it is expected. By making such a commitment and meeting the deadline, you have begun to recast accountability and support in your organization. "I will be accountable for my word. However, we all 'blow it' on occasion, and I need you both to support me (if I blow it) and be responsible for getting me what I need to perform well."

Commitment is the name of the real game; noncommitment leads to elusive, destructive games. Notice that you create by initiating your own new behavior. You create by changing your *dance.*

Step Four: Involve Your Employees in Analysis, Problem Solving, and Follow-Through

One month from now, have your employees complete the inventory and score the 25 items.[12] To ensure anonymity do not ask for names. Instead, request that they return their completed inventories in sealed envelopes

---

[12] You may choose to use the *Empowerment Profile* (Organization Design and Development, King of Prussia, PA) or a computer-scored questionnaire such as the *People Performance Profile,*™ or the *Likert Scales* (University Associates, San Diego, CA).

to your assistant or have a couple of the employees or your group tally them. There is no more powerful way to empower your group and enhance your leadership than to do this step. After reading Chapter Five, you will see that this is not turning your decision-making responsibilities over to others nor is it an easy activity the first time it is attempted. But it is the most effective way to get long-lasting change. You will find instructions in Appendix K on how to introduce this step, how to explain *why* you are doing this, and how the results will be used. For now, however, concentrate on improving the Factors on which you have scored low.

Chapter Three

Action Ideas for the 25 Factors

Factor 1 ∾ Sponsorship

Action Idea: Obtain Clear Sponsorship

The most critical factor contributing to the success or failure of a change project is the presence or absence of clear sponsorship from all managers and supervisors whose employees are involved and/or affected by the change. If any of these managers sponsor poorly, failure and increased problems are likely to occur. *A manager can only sponsor those who report to him/her!* Therefore, a department manager initiating a change must cascade sponsorship to supervisors in that department. This demands alignment of management and supervision. When such alignment is missing, front-line workers (i.e., hourlies and staff) receive conflicting messages from their respective bosses about the importance of the change and the priority of time needed to achieve the change. With unclear management alignment, matrixed task forces (i.e., with members reporting to different bosses) are seriously impaired. The changes may be technical (e.g., introduction of new computer systems or manufacturing processes), structural (e.g., mergers or re-organization), or interactive (e.g., a new empowerment emphasis).

In one organization a decision was made to pool clerical services to provide a more equitable distribution of work and more efficient coverage for absent secretaries. Many mid-managers and clerical staff opposed the move. The CEO met with his direct reports, who in turn met with mid-management to announce the decision, the implementation of the problem-solving process to be followed, and the assignment of a project consultant to guide that process. The mid-managers discussed their resistance and the anticipated resistance from the clerical staff, and then they planned for their own sponsorship with the clerical staff. Their familiar dilemma was to be in a position of saying something like: "Here's the decision that's been made. While I may not have made it this way myself because I do not like giving up my personal secretary, I fully support the decision and will back it to my utmost."

In short, the CEO made it clear that the goals and decisions were his. The employees were empowered to develop the new processes with consultant help but within the parameters set by the CEO. By making these intentions clear to mid-management and the clerical staff, he freed the consultant from persuading, coaxing, arguing, or otherwise excessively interacting with the employees, and he developed sponsorship in his mid-managers. By acknowledging their difficulty with the decision, the mid-managers maintained their integrity and yet declared their intention to support the decision.

This also positioned the mid-managers to sponsor the change effort. An effective sponsor comprehends the goals and values of the proposed change, openly wrestles with his/her concerns, monitors progress, clarifies parameters, stays open to influence, commits resources, and praises and reprimands as necessary. Such sponsoring by line management puts the consultant or change agent in a position to work with the employees. The sponsor had clarified that the goals were his, not the consultants.[13]

Sponsorship is one manifestation of participative management. Although all organizational activities have parameters, participative management devotees often lose their perspective about this. Lack of clarity about sponsorship and about parameters is a primary cause of mistrust

---

[13] Dr. Darryl Conner, ODR, Atlanta, GA, is a primary source of materials regarding sponsorship and change management.

and dysfunction. Clarity here reduces unnecessary ambiguity and greatly increases the possibilities of successful change.

Sponsorship may begin, as illustrated above, with the boss being clear about the direction (i.e., pool clerical services) but not about the implementation. Or, the boss may be unclear about both direction and implementation and may sponsor the development of a task force to develop alternatives about possible outcomes.

The most frequent error about sponsorship is the assumption by service staff (Quality, Personnel, Training, Engineering, Safety, etc.) that they can *sponsor* programs or changes throughout the organization. This misconception leads to competing priorities; change agent (engineer, trainer, chemist, quality facilitator) over-functioning (coaxing, arguing with, even *ordering* the targets of the change!); lack of single-point accountability; and foot-dragging or even failure of important projects. (For a graphic illustration of this change process, see Appendix R.)

Factor 2 ∿ Openness

Action Idea: Be Open[14]

When closed and defensive managers refer to their troublemakers, they are often referring to people who bring up problems or make suggestions. The views of these so-called troublemakers frequently represent the opinion of many others, even though the boss may believe otherwise. Defensive managers consider them to be merely griping and, thus, tend to ignore their suggestions or reprimand them, if not with words, with tone of voice and other nonverbal signals. When this happens, the so-called troublemakers either become more outspoken or they quit talking publicly and instead act covertly. Either way, everyone loses.

Of course, effective managers intend to create an open climate so that information flows overtly rather than covertly. You can change the climate

---

[14] See *An Exercise in Distinguishing Between Openness and Personal Confession,* in Appendix N.

and reduce repetitiveness from outspoken employees if you *walk your talk.* Do not expect from others what *you* do not do.

1. Decide to assume that *open resistance* is a gift that, if received well, will reduce closed or underground resistance. Resistance that has gone underground sabotages the positive energy of an organization.

2. Listen to and repeat the input so people sense that you *got their message.* For example, if an employee says, "I think we ought to have one prep cook come in an hour earlier," a paraphrase might be, "Do you mean customers are having to wait unduly for their orders?" or "Do you mean that both shifts are getting behind?" The person speaking may then confirm your paraphrase or clarify any misunderstanding and elaborate further.

   Human communication is very complex. The words we choose to convey our message usually convey, with our tone at least, a slightly different message than intended. The March 20, 1991 *New York Times* carried an article about a $500 million loss because the "Technicians at the Martin Marietta Corporation who were in charge of the Titan 3 rocket's electrical system *miscommunicated* with computer software engineers in the *same building* . . . No one was goofing off or being secretive. It was language that each group thought *meant the same thing*" (italics ours).

   Paraphrasing (the exploration of meaning) is deeper than mere parroting. Parroting is the accurate repetition of the words, and it has its place. The Navy, for example, has always recognized that messages received need to be parroted back to ensure precise understanding of the command. Paraphrasing demonstrates, however, that though we got the words, we may have missed the meaning intended.

3. Do not get hooked. In the above illustration the employee spoke for himself ("I think we ought to have . . . "). "I messages," such as "I think," "I feel," "I wish – want – agree – disagree – am concerned," etc., signify a self-differentiated person. Rational problem solving and dialogue is usually easy with this employee if the manager also has "I message" skills.

More difficult is the resistance from someone who blames, sends "you messages," or who claims to speak for all (we think, we all feel . . .). This is the language of victims, of those who take no responsibility for their situation. (See *Specificity Quiz,* Appendix G.)

In group meetings hear this person once, maybe twice. Then say, "Thank you." Look elsewhere and ask, "Who else has something?" Search for those who can engage in dialogue rather than those who operate from an emotional field. Do not turn the meeting over to the nonself-differentiated resistors.

4. Thank the others, in your own way, for caring enough to point out the problems or offer the suggestions. Tell them when you will let them know what you plan to do next and give them a "by-when" date.

5. Do not decide immediately, if your decision about a suggested solution is likely to be negative. Instead, join your employees in a search to clarify the problem and then join them in brainstorming about other possible solutions.

6. If you must totally reject the idea, do so by first paraphrasing to make sure the employee understands that you *got the idea.* Then, give your decision and explain your reason. Ask the employee to paraphrase what you have said so that you can be sure he/she *got your reason,* even if the person does not agree. The employee often will!

7. At all costs, *avoid arguing.* Your main responsibility is to get the point, respond in a timely fashion as suggested above, and share your reason. If you do this, people will regard you as being fair for listening, even if you must disagree.

8. Thank people for their suggestions. Make sure your thanks for pointing out problems or making suggestions is a separate step from whether or not you like the ideas. That is, thank people for the very *act of contributing.*

Consider the following example: A branch manager of a fast food chain restaurant was troubled by an employee turnover figure of 43%, which was 15% above the norm in the area served. The main complaint of employees was that the manager ignored all of their suggestions. After the manager was made aware of how his rejection of employee suggestions caused discontent, he vowed to be more receptive. After learning to follow the steps above, he reduced turnover to an 18% rate within two months.

Factor 3 ∽ Influence

Action Idea: Build Influence Structures

The effective manager follows what might be called a *boss and people empowerment style*. This style, in a no-nonsense way, empowers the boss(es) to be the boss and the employee to fully participate, as an employee. Bosses are not good or bad. Rather, they have an important, critical role that *cannot be denied* by pretense, lack of clarity, or cowardice. The boss *makes decisions* and puts in place effective (or ineffective) systems.

Of course, each boss has a boss. So when we say that employees must have influence and must be clear that such influence is distinctly different from the decision-making process, we mean that everyone who has a boss must have this clarity and must be empowered to influence. What do employees need to influence?

Employees need to influence:

• Clarity about my job.

• Clarity about:

> . . . any special projects I am assigned.
> . . . who decides what.
> . . . how I'm doing.

• Ability to get:

> . . . commitments from others.
> . . . the information I need to do my job.
> . . . the materials or resources needed to excel.
> . . . equipment fixed in a timely manner.

• Ability to impact productivity and quality issues.

• Ability to influence decisions that affect me, such as:

>   . . . the amount of space I have.
>   . . . the decor, ventilation, temperature, and noise in my space.
>   . . . work redesign.
>   . . . lighting, space arrangement, etc.
>   . . . procedures and processes.
>   . . . equitable compensation.
>   . . . purchases of equipment I use.
>   . . . measurements of my work.
>   . . . schedules.
>   . . . openness about what is and is not working.

That is what people need to influence. If motivation is low in your company, people may be low in influence in the above areas. If so, what can be done?

Chapter Five describes survey feedback, which, if used effectively, can help you deal with the influence needs listed above. A simple method is to ask the employees to brainstorm a list of factors inhibiting productivity/quality. (See *Brainstorm Rules,* Appendix H.) Then, follow the instructions in Appendix L. Briefly, those steps are:

1. Brainstorm inhibiting factors.

2. Encourage clarification, elaboration, and specificity.

3. Vote on priorities.

4. List specific changes desired.

5. Have boss make the decisions.

6. Act.

7. Have follow-through sessions.

Factor 4 ～ Distinguish Between Decision Making and Influence

Action Idea: Be Clear about Your Decision-Making Style

Lack of clarity about decision making and influence is a dominant cause of mistrust and low productivity. You can increase trust by being clear about who makes the decision and by understanding that there are different decision-making styles, all of which are okay. It is okay to:

1. Decide unilaterally and announce your decision. Ask for a paraphrase to make sure you have been clear.

2. *Nearly* decide, but seek council from selected/all employees prior to your final decision.

3. Describe a problem; state that you must and will decide but that first you want input, perhaps recommendations.

4. Tell the group that you will accept a majority decision even if you are outvoted. You give up veto power.

5. Go for consensus, meaning that everyone agrees that the decision is reasonable, following a thorough discussion that includes everyone's input. Again, no veto power is used.

6. Delegate the decision.

Each of these six styles carries both positive and negative consequences. The best managers learn to use them all; overuse of any one can be disastrous! Your effectiveness increases when you have clarity within yourself about which style is best for any given situation and clarity with your employees about which style you are using at any particular moment.

Effective managers most often use styles 2, 3, and 6 above. Managers of highly interdependent work groups also use approach 5, which frequently is cumbersome but encourages input and ownership of the results.

Mistrust is created when employees think you are doing what is stated in 4, 5, or 6 while you really already have decided the outcome. Managers influenced by participative management ideals often feign the use of consensus (5) when they are really being unilateral (1) or nearly so (2). People quickly catch such a discrepancy. It doesn't work; it creates mistrust.

While effective managers are careful to use it wisely, it is often necessary to use the authoritarian mode (1) in which leaders *announce* goals, visions, and directions. Most employees want to be involved in the path toward achieving the goals more than in setting the goals. When trust is high, people follow enthusiastically when leaders say, "Follow me on this path."

If overused, style 1 is totalitarianism with resulting apathy, scapegoating, and sabotage. But, used in the context of trust, of clarity about the mode being used ("I need this done today"), and of *a balance with the other styles,* it can be dynamic and visionary. Style 6, if overused and without both clear parameters and consequence management (clear reinforcement and reprimands when appropriate), will likely result in permissivism and anarchy with resulting chaos and dysfunctional performance.

Also, it is possible to use one of these styles for decision making but a different style for implementation. In Factor 1, *Obtain Clear Sponsorship,* the decision to pool secretarial resources is a style 1 decision, while the group-involvement implementation is a style 3 decision.

The following three guidelines should be applied:

1. Decide which style you will use (this will vary from situation to situation).

2. Make this choice clear to all involved.

3. Invite opinions or questions about the decision-making style you have announced. Do not defend your choice or pretend to use a style that does not seem *right* for you on this occasion.

In summary:

1.

Decide and tell	Decide after consultation and/or recommendations	Employees share in the decision	Delegate the decision (with clear parameters)
#1	#2 #3	#4 #5	#6

(Moving to the right, boss becomes less directive about outcomes.)

2. Influence increases appropriate to the employee's experience, knowledge, skill, and proven performance.

Increase of Employee Influence

3. All styles are potentially positive.

4. Effective managers mix styles. The key is to be clear about what you are doing and to be skilled in doing it.

5. Styles (2), (3) and (6) are especially important for fast-moving organizations.

6. All styles are used to achieve empowerment. (The fantasy of many empowerment programs is that only styles (5) and (6) are appropriate.)

7. Finally, all styles are participative, though each defines a different level of participation.

Factor 5 ∽ Decisions Are Made

Action Idea: Make Decisions

Before reading this read the action ideas for Factor 3, *Build Influence Structures,* and Factor 4, *Be Clear about Your Decision-Making Style.* If you have read these and still find decision making difficult, perhaps you have an analytic "make sure you have total accuracy" style or such a high concern for consensus or relationships that you wait too long to "bite the bullet."

Decision-Making Binds of Differing Styles

A high analytic style prizes attention to detail and accuracy. When things get tense and anxiety rises, such a manager seeks even more data. "I need more information," "I need to think about this," "Give me more time and I'll decide." If this description fits you, then your challenge is to take action sooner than seems right.

One such highly analytic manager decided that he would begin making decisions when he judged that 75% of the facts were in. This was very difficult for him because all of his childhood upbringing in his family and in his education to be an engineer had cultivated strong beliefs/judgments such as, "Don't be too rash," "Look before you leap," "Make sure you are right before deciding," or "Caution is the greater part of valor." While these behaviors had served him well in his engineering career, they became his "Achilles heel" when he overused them as a manager. The new, fast-moving managers above him were results-oriented. They accused him of being "nit-picky" and of "beating around the bush." Of course, such was not his intention. To develop a quicker decision-making style, he encouraged his results-oriented and spontaneous employees to push him so that he could achieve an appropriate balance between the need for accuracy and the need for making quicker decisions.

A manager with a high concern for good relationships could get stuck on not making decisions that might cause unhappiness. A hard-charging manager, on the other hand, may make decisions too quickly, without adequate details or understanding of the impact of those decisions. Such a

manager often finds her/himself reversing a previous, hastily-made decision. Spontaneous, creative managers often assume that their new idea
will excite everyone. They may *leap before they look*, with negative results.
So, all styles have value and all are sometimes misused. Versatility is the
ability to use the style that is appropriate to the moment.[15]

Factor 6 ～ Implementation

Action Idea: Implement Those Decisions

If a major change is involved, it is not enough to issue a memo or simply
publicly announce the change. With a major change you pay now or pay
later. That is, if you expect the targets of the change to gain ownership of
the change, then the planning must involve the targets significantly or the
implementation will seriously bog down or fail. For example, a large
organization initiated a major technological change by introducing a
coordinated computer system to replace dozens of systems that had
grown like topsy over the years. Such a change affects people mightily. In
this case it meant that their current system, which they developed and
understood intimately, would be altered, perhaps seriously. It could be
rendered *obsolete*. For a period of time they might not have efficient utilization of the new system. Worse yet, no one could guarantee that the
new system would ever work!

Facing the possibility of a serious disruption such as this, the targets of a
change are bound to appear resistant in the eyes of a change agent.
Change agents are those persons assigned to assist with a change. Rarely
do they have line authority. Engineers, computer technicians, quality
facilitators, and external or internal management consultants are all
examples of staff who might be change agents for different projects.
Without clear sponsorship, eventual failure is likely.

---

[15] The author has found two diagnostic tools to be particularly practical with both managers and hourly employees. Both reflect concepts similar to those described here.
These are the *U.A. Wilson Learning Social Styles,* University Associates, San Diego, CA
and the *Martin Operating Styles Inventory,* Organization Improvement Systems, El
Cajon, CA.

In the above case, the manager wisely indicated that the direction of the change was to a coordinated system, and he involved key potential users (targets) in problem-solving activities aimed at developing both an effective, detailed plan (decision about the substance of the change) *and* an effective and realistic implementation strategy.

In a previous, failed effort at another attempted major change, that same manager had hired outside experts to detail a plan. He had then attempted to train and ramrod the plan on the targets. The effort, pushed fast because of limited time, failed. The more careful involvement took longer but succeeded. Again, pay now or pay later.

Where a major change is to take place, employees need to have clear boundaries defined organizationally that spell out such practices as:

1. Except in an emergency, take orders only from your boss and not from staff members.

2. If staff members give you orders, do not quarrel. Simply inform the persons that there must be a mistake because you have not received the same orders from your boss.

3. If you think your boss is giving orders that will have a negative impact on your organization's effectiveness, say so to her/him. Be clear but not argumentative. Remember that the boss still has to "bite the bullet" and decide what he/she thinks is best.

4. If you are on staff, remember that your influence comes from four sources:

   a. Sponsor support
   b. Your communications ability
   c. Your technical expertise
   d. Your reputation.

Cultivate your skills in these four areas. You do not have legitimate line authority with anyone except those who report directly to you.

The above clarity is essential to effective implementation. Keeping boundaries creates health in families, relationships, and organizations. The change agent (staff) must always remember that the change effort or program being implemented is *not theirs* — it is the sponsor's! If they attempt to do the sponsor's work by persuading, coaxing, or threatening the targets of change, they are overfunctioning and preventing the managers from performing their proper function. Furthermore, the work will likely fail.

Factor 7 ∿ Input Needs

Action Idea: Identify Input

The *input, throughput,* and *output* process is one continual flow.

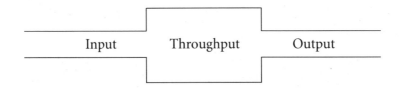

- *Input* is what is received in your department or unit.

- *Throughput* is what happens to that material, information, order, request, etc., as it moves through your unit. It is your group's work flow and processes. These are processes presumed to be the most efficient, safe, and qualitative toward producing the output expected.

- The *output* goes to your customer — internal or external.

One organization initially had each unit list the groups that had input to that unit. Then they rated the quality and the timeliness of the inputs. With this data they arranged a meeting with each supplying group. At that meeting, in a spirit of partnership, they first asked the suppliers for feedback about how they could improve their practices in order to support service from the supplier. For instance, such items as *quicker notification of their needs* and *better adherence to procedures about paperwork,* which had been neglected, were identified. Then, after demonstrating nondefensive behavior in receiving the feedback, they gave specific feedback to the suppliers.

Each group prepared by simply asking, "What do I want more of . . ., the same as . . ., or less of . . . from the other?" Clear, measurable agreements were developed and follow-through sessions were held.

Factor 8 ∼ Throughput

Action Idea: Create Effective Throughput

Once input is received, what processes within a work unit will maximize a productive, qualitative, and safe output? Time is money and therefore continuous improvement of throughput processes is essential in order to compete in the 1990s. Faster order processing, faster production, faster delivery, and faster servicing with quality is the game.

One manager developed a game board with furnaces, movable workers, and material being the input. The board was a normal desk-top size. As if engaged in a chess game, participants played the game in order to find the most effective throughput processes.

Another group developed a flow chart of the processes in their unit. While developing the flow chart of various processes, they discovered that they differed in their perceptions of what each had thought was a common perception. Once a reasonable agreement was reached about a current throughput process (including differing accounts of this reflected reality), the group then identified critical points on the flow chart. This became the base for the development of new processes.

Such new processes were regularly reviewed and revised in the heat of practice. Continuous improvement was the mindset, rather than trying to arrive at a process that would last forever. Of course, continuous improvement is only a wise course if you are already doing well. A poorly functioning group needs *rapid* improvement before being afforded the luxury of continuous improvement.

At two sister utilities, the receipt inspection was not functioning well at either location, resulting in a slower-than-desired movement of materials and parts. Of course, this resulted in delays in maintenance. Work with these groups was undertaken as a part of a departmental strategy sponsored by an unusually strong general manager. His support was a key ingredient in contributing to the initial success and the results reported below.[16]

Direct work with the groups began with separate, survey feedback sessions done at the two locations. Survey feedback (as described in Chapter 5) is a process of (1) gathering data, (2) sharing results with the work groups, (3) the work group prioritizing and conducting problem-solving sessions using the data, (4) the work group recommending actions, (5) the supervisors responding to the recommendations and making decisions (typically 90% of the recommendations are accepted), and (6) follow through. This survey feedback process addressed supervisor/ employee relations, role confusion, lack of clear accountability, intergroup dilemmas, and other dimensions related to effectiveness within the work group and between work groups. Both groups identified problems that suggested the necessity of collaboration with each other.

Upon hearing the recommendations, the department manager challenged these two groups to achieve "Order of Magnitude" improvements. He wanted them to collaborate in planning more effective business processes. They were to reduce the amount of time that material shipments lay in the warehouse undergoing inspection processes. Also, they were to standardize the inspection process and work methods between the two plants. Additionally, a one-day training in the skill of facilitation and the use of techniques for measuring and improving the quality of their work was provided to a person assigned to lead the problem-solving effort. And last, a professional facilitator was present to coach and support the fledgling facilitator. I prefer this approach to a model for training all members, which might last three to five days.

---

[16] The two groups referenced here were trained and coached by Bob and Patricia Crosby and a third consultant, Cathy Martin, all of whom were contracted through Management Analysis Company, San Diego, California. A fourth consultant, Frank (Chip) Richardson, was internal.

Increased trust in management and the ability of team members to influence had resulted from their survey feedback activity. Using skills learned in that activity, they proceeded to develop a common way of doing business for both stations by adapting the best methods from each site. They had discovered 20 areas in which they worked differently. A common system made it easier to shift inspectors between stations to meet challenging work loads.

They concluded that fundamental change would be required to reduce backlog and streamline inspection. In the past, resolving vendor error often required generating paperwork and coordinating as many as three departments outside the Receiving Group. This process often took weeks to complete while memos passed hands, deficiency reports were written, and the affected material sat unavailable in the warehouses.

Under the new methods proposed by the Team, Quality Control Inspectors began interacting daily with an on-site Material Support Team that used a new set of computer status reports to coordinate everyone involved. Inspectors began routinely to engage in instantaneous problem solving with vendors, using telecommunications equipment. Many times a shipment of deficient materials was processed for return to the vendor on the same day that it was delivered.

Implementing the Team's recommendations reduced paperwork by an estimated 30% and speeded problem resolution time-frames from several weeks to a matter of days. After additional training in measurements, the group developed ways to quantify their workloads and measure key factors. (See Factor 16.) The following results were achieved quickly:

- 20% reduction in the number of Deficiency Reports generated
- 75% reduction in the time required for a Deficiency Report disposition
- 100% reduction in the number of backlogged Deficiency Reports
- 30% reduction in overall paperwork
- 50% increase in the time inspectors actually spent inspecting.

These measurements enabled the groups to *keep their own score,* know where attention was needed, and continuously apply problem solving to improve practice.

Results such as these can only be sustained if, as noted earlier, sponsorship is strong at the top, middle, and first-line levels of management. Also, when developing team indicators, it is important to follow the guidelines mentioned in the section on Factor 16. The guidelines emphasize that the *ownership* of the data is at the work team level. Of course, nothing is sustained automatically. For all employees to take responsibility for productivity and quality, the throughput steps and principles outlined here must become a *way of life* in the organization.

Factor 9 ∿ Output

Action Idea: Get Feedback on Output

A utility company decided to develop customer feedback forms to measure output to internal customers. Aware that the proliferation of such forms would lead to reduced responses from their customers, the various units were guided in a coordinated effort.

The feedback forms were developed by the persons who were to receive the feedback. The very process of such development is confrontational. Many people resent the idea and think of it as an evaluation rather than as customer feedback. Most have not thought of other members or groups in the organization as customers. And perhaps of most importance is the fact that most service groups do not agree about what should be in the feedback form because they have *differing understandings of their jobs.* So the form development is an opportunity for the employees to become *aligned* about their task. With the boss listening well and sharing opinions in this preparation, the group will become more knowledgeable about management's expectations, and the boss will become more realistic about the employees' situation.

The feedback data is then gathered and fed back regularly for the purpose of improving service. When unsatisfactory scores surface, a simple problem-solving process can be used by the employees and boss. This requires first an analysis of the problem; second, possible solutions; and third, a plan for action.

Here are examples from two different Customer Feedback forms of internal quality groups at a utility company. The groups provided different functions. The first example lists questions from the Planning/Initial QC Interface section of a four-part form. Note how the very act of formulating these questions would help clarify the work expected of the quality inspector. Also, notice that the form uses four types of responses:

1. Yes - No questions (1a and 1b). (These are the easiest to score but are the least specific.)

2. Multiple choice (1c).

3. Scaled (1d and 1e).

4. Open-ended (1c — final two questions and Comments/ Suggestions). (Open-ended questions are difficult to score, but there is more freedom to write a response.)

Planning/Initial QC Interface

(1a) Were results of the initial phone call satisfactory?

        Yes ☐   No ☐

(1b) Did QC notification include:

    1. A discussion of QC involvement?

            Yes ☐   No ☐

    2. Scheduling of QC work and support activities?

            Yes ☐   No ☐

(1c) When requested, QC support was:

    Available   ☐   Delayed ☐

    Unavailable ☐   If delayed, why? _____

                               How long? _____

(1d) Were your specific concerns involving QC addressed?

    Adequately   Inadequately

      6   5   4   3   2   1   NA

(1e) Were QC and customer role functions clearly understood?

    Adequately   Inadequately

      6   5   4   3   2   1   NA

Comments/Suggestions concerning questions in Section I:

_____

_____

_____

From another Customer Feedback form of an audit group, here are selections from Part 3 of a five-part form.

Conduct of Audit

(3a) Assess the performance of the Auditor(s). *(Circle one number under each category.)*

   1. **Preparation**

      High   Low

      6   5   4   3   2   1   N/A

2. **Knowledge**

    High   Low

    6   5   4   3   2   1   N/A

3. **Appropriate Personnel Contacted**

    High   Low

    6   5   4   3   2   1   N/A

4. **Effective Utilization of Customers' Time**

    High   Low

    6   5   4   3   2   1   N/A

5. **Objectivity**

    High   Low

    6   5   4   3   2   1   N/A

6. **Finding(s) Discussed at Appropriate Level**

    High   Low

    6   5   4   3   2   1   N/A

7. **Communications**

    High   Low

    6   5   4   3   2   1   N/A

Factor 10 ∼ Meetings

Action Idea: Improve Meetings[17]

Meetings have a bad reputation for being frustrating time-wasters, and they deserve every bit of it. By improving the quality of meetings, you save time and improve performance. Here are some tips:

1.   Decide on the purpose of the meeting and what you want as a result. Before calling the meeting, ask if that purpose can be accomplished more efficiently by a couple of phone calls or by a memo. Often it can.

2.   Make a list of who should and who should not attend. Consider all persons on the list and the importance of their input, their biases, their concerns, and possible problems their attendance might bring. Think through how to reduce these problems, possibly by adding names to the list or removing names.

3.   Make sure someone has single-point accountability. This can be fatal when neglected in matrix meetings.

4.   Think about what meeting format will best achieve your purpose. If the purpose is strictly to convey information, presentation from the front of the room works well. If the purpose is to get agreement around an issue, a discussion format is best. For creative problem solving, include a brainstorming format.

5.   Arrange the room layout and seating so that people can see one another — not side by side but more circular. Use a board or newsprint and frequently have people write so all can see, thus making communication both visual and verbal. (See figures 1 and 1a on pages 44 and 45.

---

[17] The *Task Force Performance Profile,* Computer Profiles, Narberth, PA, has a comprehensive listing of all facets of a successful meeting. The Profile was originally co-developed with Robert Crosby in 1988.

6. Begin the meeting by reviewing the agenda and get clarity about the scheduled time. Pace the meeting to cover all key agenda items.

7. Freely appoint small task groups to do further work on various items rather than waste time with long, total group discussions.

8. Avoid two-person, private discussions. When two people get into a conversation not relevant to the others, suggest that they finish the conversation later. But if all need to hear this particular discussion, let it continue.

9. Encourage participation by all. If only three or four talk out of a group of ten, ask the quiet persons for their ideas. Or, try something new — arrange participants into pairs or triads for as little as two to three minutes. Instructions can be as simple as, "Talk to your partner about this subject. I'll give you three minutes and then you'll report the discussion." Encourage people to pair with someone they haven't had much opportunity to talk with recently.

10. Record commitments and action items. Have someone record on newsprint (for all to see) who is to do what and by when following the meeting. Be alert for statements like, "I'll look into that." Such statements, sounding like action, often go unrecorded. Make clear who is to do what and by when.

11. Before the meeting ends, review decisions, agreements, and who will do what by when (action items). (See Factor 20.)

12. Begin the next meeting by reviewing the action items agreed to at the previous meeting. When breakdowns occur, find out why and fix them.

Who is the best person to lead the meeting? The answer may surprise you — it is often *not* the boss. Being the boss is, of course, a critical role, but leading (being a meeting facilitator) is a separate role. Combining these two is sometimes difficult. For one thing, bosses rarely carefully plan a meeting, except for the agenda. A skilled facilitator designs the information-giving part of the meeting to include paraphrase activities, comments, and questions in order to maximize clarity through two-way rather than one-way communication.

The problem-solving portion of the meeting includes small-group activities with guidance about problem-solving steps in order to create both higher quality and ownership of the eventual solutions. The functions of being boss (the authority figure) and facilitator (the process guider) are separate. Though they may be performed by the same person, the boss is freer to participate if he/she grants the authority to lead to a facilitator.

If your meetings occur in a noisy plant setting rather than a quieter office setting, you will need to modify these steps. Your meetings may be stand-up, 10-minute sessions with machine noise in the background. Do not just ask, "Are there any questions?" Rather, tell people to talk for a couple of minutes with someone standing beside them. Get people involved and they will become more responsible; pass the ball to them. This takes courage. The high talkers resist paired conversations as do the low talkers, but for different reasons. Both want to maintain the status quo with most members avoiding responsibility.

These suggestions should help to make your meetings crisper and more effective. In turn this will save time, increase accountability, and boost performance.

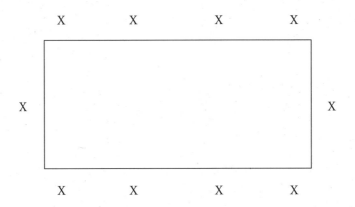

Fig. 1. Patriarchal/matriarchal arrangement.

In this arrangement people seated side by side cannot see each other. Attention is primarily focused on the head of the table.

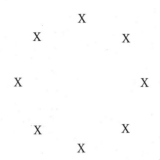

Fig. 1a. Participation arrangement.

With a participation arrangement people can see each other better and notice head nods and facial responses. They can bring into the conversation quieter members who have tried to enter but backed off in deference to more outspoken members. This gatekeeping function (opening the gate for others to enter) is a role that all members should assume, not just the leader. There is evidence to support the notion that those who do not participate, even if they agree with the proceedings, are less committed to action than are more active members.

Factor 11 ∼ Creativity

Action Idea: Build a Climate for Creativity

High performance occurs when people are comfortable contributing creative ideas. Some things that you can do to stimulate creativity:

1. As with openness, thank people for independent thought whether or not you agree with the particular idea. Separate the "thanks" from your response to the idea.

2. Enrich the quality of meetings by including brainstorming. Excellent brainstorming can be accomplished in a few minutes. Encourage brainstorming while faithfully following the rules of brainstorming:[18]

---

[18] See Appendix H.

3. Encourage bold, expansive ideas. Where wild ideas occur (such as "take a moon trip and send the name of our product to earth by laser beam"), guide a discussion looking for the kernel of truth in the wild idea. Press people to find practical applications of fantasy ideas.

4. Pause to let each individual write private thoughts. If a group is *rationally* trying to produce a written product, have each person spend time alone writing and then come back together. Or, you may have them create an abstract picture, explain it, and derive implications for the needed written product.[19]

    Success of the innovative Macintosh computer is credited to the Apple team, which encouraged, even insisted, on bold and wild ideas during their development meetings.

5. Stop by Mary's office to tell her that you heard her marketing plan for Product X didn't work out well. Thank her for being creative about such plans. Encourage her to keep inventing and assure her of your support.

6. To John, the salesman who had a bad week, express appreciation for his effort, reflect that he certainly has had some good weeks, and ask if there is anything innovative that he would like to try. Perhaps he has seen you as conservative and needs your support for a change to occur.[20]

---

[19] See *C&RT*, a creative risk taking measurement, by Richard Byrd, University Associates, San Diego, CA. Helps identify individuals who may be "innovators," those who are "synthesizers," etc., in your organizations. All are important to an organization.

[20] See *The "I" of the Hurricane: Creating Corporate Energy*, by Art McNeil, Stoddart Publishers, 1986, Canada. Useful for many practical illustrations of "signals."

Factor 12 ∾ Job Clarity

Action Idea: Clarify Roles/Jobs

Concern regarding the clarity of roles/jobs may reflect the following:

1. Confusion between the understood job assignment and what one is asked to do.

2. Confusion about prioritization of tasks.

3. Orders from many sources, such as other bosses or staff (engineering, quality, safety, senior employees).

4. Confusion by others about one's task, leading to requests for help outside of one's understood role.

In a large organization work teams at the hourly level were asked, "What do you do and what should the job include?" Supervisors then reported the responses to their managers in a joint session and listed on large newsprint sheets *possible duplications* and *possible gaps* as they heard the reports. A discussion ensued with decisions made confirming, adding to, or deleting functions. This was then reported back to each group by the supervisor. This process continued *up* the organization using the same process with the top management team. (See Appendix C for an illustration of one group's final product, *Role Clarity*.)

Within this organization there were 14 engineering functions located in various departments; 50 possible duplications were identified, of which 12 were later considered to be actual dysfunctional duplications of work; 15 possible gaps were identified, of which 8 were deemed important and yet had not been assigned anywhere in the organization.

Involving the people who do the daily work is the most effective way both to develop living role assignments and to provide management with an opportunity to make decisions about the best placement of tasks. This also informs all persons about their roles.

Factor 13 ⌒ Person-Task Fit

Action Idea: Make Sure There Is a Person/Task Fit

Work groups function best when their members can do what they do well and enjoy doing. Of course, it is not possible to achieve a perfect match all the time. Some routine, uninspiring tasks need to be done that, while requiring excellence, do not require our best talent. But, it is often possible to adjust tasks in the work group to create a better person/task fit. To test whether members of your work group are underutilized, have each one fill in the chart in figure 2. After each person fills out the chart, review it with him/her. The significance of the boxes is described in figure 3.

With your team examine the possibilities for shifting work around or doing it differently. Discussing these items together as a team is more effective than simply having the boss and one employee discuss them. Team planning can lead to trading of tasks and cross-training so people can support each other better.

	Things I do best	Things at which I am less skilled
Things I am asked to do often		
Things I am not often expected to do		

Fig. 2. Task/person fit matrix.

	Things I do best	Things at which I am less skilled
Things I am asked to do often	Excellent fit. Productivity possibility is high.	Poor fit. Productivity possibility low unless you plan for: 1. Training 2. Transfer these tasks to someone else.
Things I am not often expected to do	Potential fit. Productivity possibility is high if you plan for: 1. These tasks to be transferred to this person. 2. This person to rotate jobs more frequently.	Leave as is or: 1. Reduce further expectations to do these. 2. Training to move these diagonally (top left quadrant) for organizational benefit or individual growth and challenge.

Fig. 3. Task fit explanation.

Factor 14 ∾ Authority

Action Idea: Clarify Authority

In the *People Performance Profile* diagnostic tool there is a question that reads, "If given responsibility for a task, I also have authority to do it."[21] This question is scored under the category *Job Satisfaction,* which has six subcategories including *Authority.*

Frequently this subcategory scores the lowest among hourly workers, staff, and mid-managers. In one organization this problem was addressed as follows:

1. Each of the three groups referenced above was asked to specify areas of ambiguity about authority.

2. Appropriate managers clarified who had authority to do what. With some groups an authority matrix was developed, such as the following:

Work issue	Who decides?	Who is consulted prior to decision?	Who carries out the action?
1.			
2.			
3.			
4.			
5.			
Etc.			

There are many variations of this chart. Other columns included have headings such as: Who has single-point accountability? Who is to be informed?

---

[21] The data is from the *People Performance Profile* (PPP).™

3. Hourlies were trained not to take orders from staff or other bosses except under special or emergency conditions. They were encouraged to say, "I'm sorry, but my boss has not indicated that this is a task that I am to do."

4. Simultaneously, staff were trained not to give orders or otherwise attempt to manipulate the hourly workers. Their task was to ensure appropriate sponsorship (see Factor 1). Thus, if they met with resistance from the hourly workers, they were instructed to report their surprise at the (apparent) lack of clear sponsorship and to return to their bosses with this information of (apparent) non-alignment. Such training of staff (quality facilitators, engineers, chemists, and other staff specialists) can bring much clarity into an organization. The authority of support staff lies in their technical expertise, interpersonal skills, and their ability to help the organization be clear about who is sponsoring the activity. Staff members do not have programs — sponsors do. The staff helps others achieve their goals.

Only when there is such clarity will hourlies, staff, mid-managers, first-line supervisors, and top management have the authority each needs to be effective.

Factor 15 ～ Resource Availability

Action Idea: Make Sure That Resources Are Available

> "I can't get the information I need to do my job."
> "Materials are not available when needed."
> "Repairs/breakdowns are not handled in a timely manner."
> "I can't get what I need from other groups."

No one has to be persuaded that this portends disaster. What can be done about it? First, it is essential to understand that these are systems issues and that they demand systems responses. A systems issue is simply one that crosses the entire organization in its operation and its impact. It cannot be corrected by only materials management staff. It certainly cannot be corrected by expert outside consultation, better training, or new management even though all of these may, at the appropriate time, be helpful.

To tackle this issue successfully both key hourly workers *and* decision makers must be involved. How? Decision makers free the key involved workers from various units across the site to devote intense, problem-solving time to this task. At one utility, a serious systems issue like this was solved by involving staff from such units as materials management, design and systems engineering, quality assurance, and maintenance. Each organization assessed who the key players were and released them for this task.

Led by a skilled facilitator through a guided problem-solving activity, this ad hoc group produced a product in a week that solved a systems issue that had been festering and delaying production for months. (See *Characteristics of an Effective Facilitator,* Appendix J.)

The guidance of a facilitator is essential. Such a person must know problem-solving steps, conflict utilization, and have the authority (both personal and organizationally-granted) to move the group. The facilitator should be both neutral about substantive outcomes and skilled in guiding a change process.

A good design includes ways to inform key bosses of the group's direction and ways to keep the dialogue current between the decision makers and the problem solvers. The workers must know the parameters within which they are working so as not to be blindsided by having their recommendations stonewalled. Bosses should not be involved in the problem solving unless they are a *worker* with key information. By all means the facilitator must guide the process.

Follow-through, including by-whens, must be thorough. On complex issues follow-through will continue for months and may include the working out of new emerging issues by subgroups of the original group. Some aspects of the original solution may prove weak and need additional work.

One plant had not succeeded on a technical task despite nine months of effort. They had over 100 widgets to complete and had not completely finished any (including paperwork). After an in-depth session involving 40 workers and 20 decision makers at appropriate levels, the plant finished 78 widgets in the next three months.

In the group you manage the solution may be simpler. Once people identify the unavailable resources or otherwise specify the problems, you can then bring together the key players.

But remember — do not play superperson and try to solve the problem yourself or with just one employee. If it is a systems issue, as many resource availability problems are, grant the time needed to let those key players work through the issue with skilled help. It will save time and money in the long run.

Factor 16 ∼ Team Measurements

Action Idea: Develop Team Measurements[22]

Workers in a food industry identified a can labelling problem as a major bottleneck. They did this after developing indicators to measure both their output and input. For input they began to track cans coming to their three lines from the work team responsible for that function. They also tracked maintenance of equipment as an input item. Through a joint agreement with maintenance, their goals were to reduce downtime on equipment, increase planned and predictable needed maintenance, decrease the time required for them to notify maintenance when breakdowns occurred, and improve communication and relationships with maintenance employees. All of these are measurable; some are direct and some indirect, but all are measurable.

In addition, they began to measure the flow of cans on each line during each shift through their labelling function. Such measurements then enabled them to track and solve problem items that scored lower or higher than desired.

---

[22] The author acknowledges the contributions over the past several years of Dr. Gerald Swanson, Frank "Chip" Richardson, and Michael Snodgrass.

The following guidelines are key toward developing such team indicators:

1. Choosing what is to be measured is a shared activity.

2. Measurement is used for improvement — not punishment.

3. Measurement devices are kept simple.

4. Groups compete with their own goals, not with other groups.

5. Measurement is comprehensive rather than evaluating a single item.

6. Measurement belongs to the group.

7. Measurement is not designed to develop an aggregate score across the entire organization.

8. Results are reported frequently.

Note: The Appendix has illustrations of plant-wide (macro) and department indicators that need to be known so that work teams can develop measurements that are specific to their responsibilities.

The following are simple steps to guide a work team in the development of its own measurements (micro). These, in addition to the macro and departmental indicators, help employees to know the *score* and to become an important part of the team.

The first step is to help groups identify their customers, that is, who do they serve within their organization? Then, recalling their most successful day, have them describe their output to their customer. Following this, groups are then ready to see the Direct/Indirect Productivity Measurement lists. Because these items are from many businesses, some will be irrelevant. The list will serve as a stimulus. Have them circle the items that apply to them and add new items that are directly relevant to the work group.

Direct Productivity Measurements

Increases

Net profit
Gross sales
Field sales
Number of units produced
Number of billable hours
Market penetration
Forecasting accuracy
New members
New clients
Program attendance
Pledged money
Schedule attainment
Units shipped per day

Reductions

Accident rate
Workmen's compensation claim rate
Absenteeism rate
Medical costs
Turnover
Shrinkage rate
Equipment repairs
Union grievances
Customer complaints
Warranty costs
Recall rate
Re-working rate
Average time to process claims
Empty bed days
Costs per patient day
Recidivism
Cost per case
Hydraulic oil usage
Electricity (kilowatts per engine)
Design change rate
Stock outs per week
Average time to fill vacancies
Damaged goods

Number of incomplete work packages
Average time between receiving materials
    and green tagging by quality
Number of times stock items run out
    before being reordered
Number of items incorrectly listed in
    nucleus (computer system)
Number of vendor complaints
Procedures violation in-house
Number of incomed P.O.'s
Number of blanket orders returned
Number of P.O.'s returned for
    inadequate item description
Number of Priority One items
    never picked up from warehouses
Maintenance supplies per engine
Re-tooling and re-run rates
Reject parts or units rate
Down time
Late deliveries
Shop development time
Overdue shop orders
Daily scrap
Maintenance labor per engine

Indirect Measurements

Increases	Reductions
Trust	Wasted time
Role Clarity	Carelessness
Teamwork	Sabotaging
Loyalty and commitment	Anger and fear
Creativity	Stalling
Job satisfaction	Defensiveness
Personal caring	Personal stress
Pride in work	Interference with work
Follow-through	Rumor-mill communication
Administrative efficiency	Ineffective meetings
Accurate, clear communication	Low self-esteem
Quality decision-making	Confusion about rules and procedures
Confidence in planning	Production/marketing conflict
Feeling productive	Sales/service conflict
Effective time management	Feedback from customer
Responsiveness to change	
Personal health	
Nutritional awareness	
Outreach	

Next, using the multi-voting guidelines (see Step 5 of Appendix L), select important measurements. Using a line graph or bar graph (the macro measures in Appendix D illustrate both), plan for measurement. Also, plan for how you will gather the data, display it (private or public), and apply the problem-solving process to the items that are rated lower than you wish. It is likely that several employees will have skills in working with measurements and graphs and would enjoy this responsibility.

In follow-through sessions celebrate items that are scored high and work on solving those items that are scored low.[23] Also, keep asking, "Is that

---

[23] The problem-solving steps in Chapter 5, "Survey Feedback — Turning Data Into Action," may help here.

measurement still important? Do we need to add another measurement?
Are our goals high enough? Is there a better way to gather data?"

The discerning reader will understand that this will help to sharpen
employee involvement. Problem solving will be focused on trying to raise
the scores. Also, it will be clear when it is appropriate to celebrate success.

The manager's role in this process is important. While all concerned will
participate, the manager must concur that indeed the measurements used
actually do measure those areas assigned to this work team.

Although line and bar graphs may be simpler and easier for most to
understand, we have found considerable interest in a matrix scoring
method developed by the Oregon Productivity and Technology Center.[24]
Some work teams prefer a display like the Indicators Matrix that follows.

---

[24] See the *Department Performance Indicators,* Appendix D, for an illustration of this
   matrix

Indicators Matrix

Step 1. Major criteria impacting productivity in a given area are identified, appropriate measures determined for each, and the resultant monitors entered in the boxes slanted across the top.

Step 2. The current level of performance in the area is calculated for each criterion and the ensuing numerical results entered at a level corresponding to a score of 3. (Note the scores listed vertically at the right of the Matrix.)

Step 3. Based on broad organizational goals, productivity objectives are established for all criteria. These quantitative targets are entered at a level corresponding to a score of 10.

Step 4. Step-wise goals, or mini-objectives, are then determined and the squares from score levels 3 to 10 are filled in with these successive "hurdles."

Step 5. At the same time, flexibility to account for tradeoffs or occasional slack periods is recognized, and figures are inserted in the squares below score level 3. Quotients associated with anything less than minimum likely performance correspond to a score of 0.

	TIME-LINESS Late Orders / Total Orders	EQUIP-MENT Machine Downtime / Scheduled Hours	WASTE Pounds Waste Out / Pounds Received	PRODUC-TION Total Units Out / Total Labor Hours	SAFETY 5 x Frequency plus Severity	QUALITY Defective Units / Total Units Out		Productivity Criteria
Row A	5.5%	16%	13.25%	605	320	9.5%		**Performance**
Step 3	0	0	10	800	0	0		..10
	.2	2	11	770	50	3		..9
	.5	4	12	740	125	5		..8
	1	6	13	710	175	7		..7
	2	8	(14)	680	225	9		..6
	3	10	15	650	275	(11)		..5
	4	12	16	620	(325)	13		..4
Step 2	5	14	17	(590)	375	15		..3
	(6)	(16)	18	560	390	17		..2
	7	18	19	530	405	19		..1
Step 5	8	20	20	500	420	21		..0
Row B	2	2	6	3	4	5		**Score**
	5	10	20	30	15	20	**Step 6**	**Weight**
Row C	10	20	120	90	60	100		**Value**

Step 4 — Scores

Step 7 | Index **400**

Step 6. Since some criteria are more important than others, weightings are assigned to each. The sum of these weights equals 100 and can be distributed in any informative fashion (see Weight row). This step defines the productivity mission of the area in question.

Step 7. At the conclusion of every monitoring period, the actual measure for each criterion is calculated and placed in the "performance" boxes on Row A. The level that these achievements represent is then circled in the body of the Matrix and associated with a score of from 0-10. Scores are entered in the appropriate box on Row B at the bottom of the Matrix. Each score is then multiplied by the weight for that same criterion, to obtain a value, listed on Row C. The sum of all values yields a productivity index for the period. Over time, the movement of this single index tracks the net results of productivity efforts in the area of interest.

For a complete understanding of the above matrix, refer to *Productivity by the Objectives Matrix* (Autumn, 1983), published by the Oregon Productivity and Technology Center, an extension of the College of Business at Oregon State University, Corvallis, OR.

Factor 17 ∼ Big-Picture Perspective

Action Idea: Paint the Big Picture

Have you ever dictated a letter to a secretary and been asked numerous questions about your intent? Most secretaries cannot type well without understanding the context or content. Secretaries who understand the larger picture see more effective ways to communicate the intent and even can suggest slight shifts that will improve a letter.

Most people need to understand the larger picture of a task, of their work unit, of the company, of the industry, or of the world scene as it relates to the task at hand.

When your team sees the big picture of your goals, the risks, and the market opportunity, both they and you win by being more effective. Here are some ways to help people clearly see the big picture:

1. Tell them the background behind a task. Share information about what the customer is looking for. Share the history of past successful or failed efforts to achieve the same outcome. This helps people to repeat successes and avoid failures.

2. Be brief; touch key themes and allow for questions. Err on the side of allowing time for questions rather than talking too long. Realize that people differ in what they need to know to complete *their* picture. Some want more details about *how* it will work. Some want to know *why* it is important. Others want to know *what* good it will do; *what* will result from doing it. And, others want to know *who* suggested it or *who* has tried it before.

    Do not guess what others want to hear. Their questions will make that clear to you. There is no way that an extended speech by you, without questions, will achieve the same results. If you ask the classic question, "Are there any questions?" and get the classic response, "No" or "Just one," reread the eighth suggestion for improving meetings.

3. Encourage employees to clip newspaper and magazine articles that are directly or indirectly related to your industry. Provide a prominently placed bulletin board for such clippings.

4. Describe the larger picture about your company's products.[25] For example:

    a. *Market trends:* Who used to buy our products? How were they distributed? How has that changed? How will it change? One large food processing company had as its consumer, a generation ago, the small grocery store customer. By 1985, their primary consumer was the fast food industry.

    b. *Cultural history:* Who started the company? How did they handle crises? How were decisions made? How is that the same or different now?

    c. *Mission statements:* Note how the mission of the food processing company mentioned above would, of necessity, have had to shift with its shifting market. Now the customers, i.e., fast food chains, visit the plant, meet the workers, and see the production processes.

    d. *Competitive strategy and competitors:* The market shift for the food processing company called for a different strategy than was needed when the primary customers were grocery stores and individual consumers.

---

[25] See Factor 18 for an example of a training activity to assist managers in communicating the big picture.

Factor 18 ～ Training

Action Idea: Provide for Relevant Just-in-Time Training[26]

Employees in a manufacturing plant complained that technical training was either missing or poorly done. After surveying employees in order to develop a multiple choice list, employees and management prioritized the list.

Highly-skilled employees were then nominated to lead training experiences. Some were 30-minute sessions; others lasted for several hours. Many sessions took place on the plant floor at the machine of the trainer and/or the trainees. A stipend was paid for doing the training. Sessions were informal with a hands-on emphasis. This was only one variable in an extensive organizational development strategy, but it surely contributed to the remarkable gains in the marketplace made by this particular firm.

Another organization trained all the managers to (1) state the current market situation and the current business objectives, and (2) declare to their teams their individual expectations of their specific role toward the achievement of those objectives.

Using video replay, managers were pushed to speak in "I" rather than "we" or "they" language. "Here's what I need and expect!" Many managers reveal a lack of personal commitment by saying "they want" or "the company wants."

Furthermore, *no* generalities were allowed. When a manager said, "I want you to take good care of the machines," he/she was pushed to be specific about what people were to do that he/she would evaluate as "taking good care." Words like *initiative* and *cooperation* were translated to specificities. This positioned the manager to communicate better both the big picture and the specific, important role of her/his group. In an anonymous evaluation, 42 managers rated this training a 9.1 in *practicality* (1 to 10 scale, 10 being high).

---

[26] See comments about training on page 83, Chapter 4.

Just in time is an important principle for training. This managerial training immediately preceded meetings with the managers' direct reports. Most training loses its effectiveness because it does not immediately precede the moment of use.

For example, large companies, often confusing activities with results, will report that 1500 people were trained in the past year in quality or communication or problem-solving processes. So what! What were the results? Reread the receipt inspection story in the throughput activity (pages 36-38.) This quality process was led by an employee who had just received a *one-day* facilitation training. The other participating employees had received *no* training. However, a skilled coach was present to help this novice facilitator lead his first quality process. In his department no one could be trained unless he or she had a facilitation assignment that would begin immediately after the training . . . *just in time!*

The managers referenced above had been previously trained in conflict management. In that training participants increased their ability to deal with differences, to appreciate behavioral styles opposite of their own, to speak for themselves *(I want, I think, I feel)* or, when accurate, to say *we.* Also, the training had included an exploration of family patterns for dealing with differences so that participants could decide whether or not to continue to (like a knee-jerk) repeat dysfunctional patterns. Such training helps participants *differentiate* between themselves and others, be less reactive, and be more of a choice-maker about responses to others rather than a seeming victim whose constant excuse is, "I did this because they did that."[27]

---

[27] LIOS, The Leadership Institute of Seattle, founded by Bob Crosby in 1969, has a key ingredient built around *self-differentiation* in its consulting work and its MA program in the Applied Behavioral Sciences. LIOS director, Brenda Kerr, Dennis Minno (current faculty member), and Dr. Ron Short (former faculty member) developed these concepts and built training designs. They give credit to Dr. Edwin Friedman and his mentor, Dr. Murray Bowen, for their original ideas in this area. LIOS, 1450 114th Ave. SE, Suite 230, Bellevue, WA 98004. The author, along with Dr. Ron Short and John Scherer were the original faculty of the MA program, which began in 1973. The Crosbys are current faculty members.

Factor 19 ∿ Priorities

Action Idea: Set Priorities

"Priorities aren't clear" is a familiar refrain. Often it means, "I have too many bosses." The lower down the organization hierarchy, the more likely it is that the employee will:

- be told what to do by several people.
- be asked to do things beyond the job description.
- find it difficult to say "no" or draw appropriate boundaries.
- feel stressed and victimized.

Appropriate boss behavior is to make clear to everyone that:

- the boss is responsible for setting priorities.
- the job description and expectation of the employee is . . .
- the employee is instructed, when asked by someone else to do something that seems to be outside the job expectations, to ask that person to talk to the boss.
- the employee, when overloaded, is expected to check priorities with the boss.

Another frequent situation is when employees complain that their boss does not set priorities. Some bosses are not good at this even if people think they should be because they are in the *boss position*. The boss may be less experienced or a very analytically-oriented person who overdoes the seeking of further data before deciding. (See Factor 5, *Decision Making*.) I have seen the following approach work on many occasions:

Choose the employee who is best at prioritizing, and get an agreement from this employee that at an appointed time each day or week, he/she will submit a prioritized list to the boss for approval. Many bosses are relieved at this suggestion. It is okay not to be good at everything!

Factor 20 ∼ By-Whens

Action Idea: Clarify By-Whens

The key statement, "When we leave a meeting, it is clear who will do what and by when," scored a 1.12 on a six-point scale in a recent survey *(People Performance Profile)*. That is not unusual; change here can be dramatic. A score of 1.12 can become a 4+ score quickly.

To change this, focus on your meetings — the formal ones as well as those informal, stand-up sessions. Meetings are a hologram of your larger organization. That is, the meeting is a focused story of what probably is happening in the organization. Starting now, have someone note every commitment and record by when it will be completed. *It is not a commitment without a by-when.* "Someday" or "hopefully" is *not* a commitment. Do not let anyone say, "I'll have it for you, if I get it from Joe." Someone *must* say, "I'll make sure it happens!" There must be a single-point accountability.

Before the meeting is dismissed, review the commitments; three or four out of every ten may be disputed. "I said that?" Be sure the commitments are clear. Negotiate more realistic time commitments, if necessary. Make it clear that the next meeting will begin by reviewing the commitments made at the last meeting.

One group of managers wore pins that read, "Ask me for a by-when." The right to ask must go up the organization, laterally, and down. Furthermore, whoever asks has that concern on his/her front burner and should be empowered to support (remind?) the by-when giver when breakdowns occur. The example of the boss *giving* by-whens is the pacesetter. The goal is to *make it happen.*

Factor 21 ∼ Follow-Through

Action Idea: Commit to Follow-Through

Action is usually the goal of a meeting. What causes action? Most groups believe that if they make a good decision, they have acted, or if everyone is in favor of something, or if they have achieved true consensus or if everyone is involved in the process, action will follow. Maybe. Probably not.

Factor 20 highlighted the critical by-when dimension. But, commitment is even more basic to follow-through. Only commitment leads to action. If you get action on something, anything, it means you had commitment to do it. If no action followed, you had no commitment. In other words, the level of commitment can be assessed by looking at results. People do the things to which they are committed. If nothing happens after a group has made a decision, then the group was committed to doing nothing when the meeting ended.

Two Kinds of Commitment

1. *"I'll try. . ."* commitment. The overall result is usually less success, less empowerment, feelings of helplessness and frustration by the group, and defensive behavior characterized by blaming.

2. *"No matter what . . ."* commitment. This is characterized by dedication to achieving the results promised, not taking "no" for an answer, or not letting anything stop you from making good on your word. There are always other forces in a situation, but a real commitment says, "I will not let anything stop me. If I fail to carry this out, I will take responsibility. I will not make excuses but will apply problem solving to maximize future success." Organizations need to be the kind of place where people give their word and others can count on it.

In one organization, scheduling was in disarray in the unit that received trucks bringing raw material and dispatched trucks delivering finished products. The members of the unit made commitments to give and ask for a by-when from one another. When this became an internal unit practice, trucks started to arrive and leave on schedule as if a miracle had happened! The surprised workers realized that even without an organized campaign, their new way of communicating had also become standard with their truck drivers.

"If I commit to do something and see that I have overcommitted, I will tell you. We will work together to determine what to do." This is not about self-flagellation. Commitment is about my giving my word so that action will happen in a more predictable way. It is about organizational effectiveness.

More About Commitment

Commitment is taking risks. Using words like "try" or "probably" may feel like you are keeping an out for yourself . . . but not really. Everyone knows the bluff . . . down deep.

How can you be sure enough to make a commitment? You can't. Commitment is *not* about being sure — it is about having guts. It is *not* playing safe; it is going after the stakes even when you could be wrong.

What if I "blow" a commitment? You will! Only those who *play it safe* never blow a commitment. Commitment is about taking a risk — it means committing to a "possible possibility." When it becomes apparent that you are not going to make your commitment, you must notify the appropriate person(s). Perhaps he/she can make available to you the material or people support needed to get your commitment back on track. His/her response will be, "Thanks for telling me. How can I support you in getting this done by the commitment time or as soon as possible?" "What is your new commitment time?" And, when you call, you say simply, "I blew it." No excuses. Do not meet people *as an excuse giver.*

The above is greatly assisted when you say, "I'll get back to you by (when)" or "What do you need from me and by when?" Then you can begin to say with personal and not just boss authority, "By when will you have that on my desk?"

Only by modeling this behavior and then expecting it from others will this culture be created . . . not by memo or preaching . . . but by your word. *You and your employees will be able to count on each other's word.* Schedules will be met, budgets will be accurate, trucks will arrive on time, and a new energy will flow in the place you are creating. This is an ideal state for which we all should constantly strive. Like freedom, it takes constant vigil.

Factor 22 ∼ Single-Point Accountability

Action Idea: Identify Single-Point Accountability

This is a serious problem wherever there is a matrixed task force or matrixed organization. Who is accountable? Not me. Them. The group. Nobody, because we were matrixed. Matrixed refers to people working on a common task (short-term or long-term) who report to different bosses.[28] "I couldn't get this report completed because the engineers didn't give me their estimates on time." This is the classic finger-pointing opportunity. What to do?

The bosses clarify among themselves in whose department the single-point accountability will lie. Each boss then communicates this to his/her representative in the matrixed group. At a subsequent meeting, the primary sponsoring boss meets with the group and clarifies his/her expectations with all concerned:

> "Joe has single-point accountability. I have cleared this with all of your bosses. Have you all been informed?" (If not, then, "I'll be calling your boss(es) immediately after I leave here to find out what went amiss.") "I'll check with Joe weekly. This task is important to me. I expect it to be completed by __(date)__, with a mid-term milestone on__(date)__. Joe's assignment is to handle absences, tardiness, unmet by-whens, and other relevant problems you are having without overfunctioning. That is, if he cannot work it out easily with you, then I expect him to report that problem to me so I can fix it quickly. That puts him in a difficult position if you are not succeeding. But, that is exactly what I expect of him. I do not take this task lightly. Any questions?"

---

[28] The *Task Force Performance Profile* is a meeting questionnaire especially for matrixed task forces often led by project managers in large organizations.

If a matrixed group is not important enough to demand such clarity or sponsorship, why have it? The intent behind identifying single-point accountability is to eliminate the black hole where *nobody* is responsible for essential functions. In a *make-it-happen* context this is empowering. (See Chapter One.) Reward people for success and even for stepping up and making the commitment . . . "I'll handle that." When it appears that someone has not succeeded, make it clear that you appreciate his/her intentions and that you now have to apply some problem-solving efforts to the apparent dilemma, with the goal of ensuring success. If reprimands are necessary, do so as suggested in Factor 24. As a manager, spread the majority of your accountabilities singly and specifically across your direct reports. If they, in turn, have direct reports, they should do the same.

This concept, single-point accountability, is frequently misunderstood. Some assume it is simply a clerical tracking function. Others assume that this implies one who can make all the decisions. These are extreme positions. The person with single-point accountability is a *proactive* task manager who is point-person about the ongoing status of the task and who insists on clarity about decision making among the various components of the project. A decision matrix is critical (see the Action Idea for Factor 14). This person is highly skilled as a change agent and therefore knows how to ensure clear sponsorship, by-whens, and follow-through. This person knows when to handle an issue with peers and when the issue is one of sponsorship (i.e., unclear scope, roles, resource allocation, or prioritites).

Factor 23 ∼ Reinforcement

Action Idea: Reinforce Success

The most fundamental principle of psychology is this: What is rewarded today will be done tomorrow. Yet, too often the story is, "Around here you only hear what you've done wrong." Here are some ways to reinforce success:

1. Reward exceptional performance by giving individuals or groups:

    *   a chance to work with equipment that they have wanted to use.

    *   a chance to do a task or a project that excites them. These may uncover a growing edge for your company that you weren't sure should be explored.

    *   budgetary support for a special project or for their ongoing work.

    *   assignment of preferred work partners.

    *   paid trips to professional meetings.

    *   relief from repetitive tasks.

2. Encourage your organization to develop a gain-sharing program to share the fruits of productivity/quality improvement.

3. Ask employees to point out examples of exceptional performance that may go unnoticed by peers or management. Your company has its share of invisible heroes whose day-by-day *going beyond the call of duty* performances are probably taken for granted. Acknowledge these people. Celebrate together!

4. Celebrate high performance with dinners, barbecues, a cake at break, balloons, roses, a hula-dance, etc. Let your people have fun and let off steam. It is good for business.

The manager of a high-quality clothing store realized that he tended to highlight mistakes his salespeople made but seldom pointed out what they did well. He decided that he would *positively reinforce* his employees by the following actions:

1. *He commended.* On a door that all walked through, he pasted notes calling attention to excellent performances by his sales staff.

2. *He encouraged.* "Joe, I just thought about that promotion you suggested yesterday. Thanks for the idea. Could you expand on that idea?"

3. *He gave positive feedback.* "Mary, I see you had some big sales yesterday. Nice going!"

4. *He rewarded.* "Tom, I noticed that your shift tagged the sales merchandise in record time. I'll bring in some Danish pastry tomorrow and thank them."

Another manager described his philosophy as follows:

1. Reward results, not effort.

2. Give rewards in a timely way.

3. Reward teams rather than individuals if you are encouraging teamwork.

4. Make sure people know the specific result(s) for which they are getting rewarded.

5. Do all of the above in the context of the strategies designed to achieve the values and business objectives. That is, reinforce activities that help achieve the desired organizational direction.

This manager made an effort to reinforce positively. He kept reinforcement simple, made it genuine, and used it daily.

Factor 24 ∼ Reprimands

Action Idea: Reprimand Poor Performance

Reprimands are inevitable. They may be inferred through facial grimaces, a negative tone, the silent treatment, gossip reported by another employee, or praise withheld. Through generalized judgments (e.g., you are not showing initiative), the employee may have seen more evidence of the boss' displeasure. Some employees have experienced bosses who *suddenly* lose their temper. Perhaps the explosion of anger included a dismissal.

Leading to all of the above, the boss' expectations had not been met. Also, none of the above clearly specified the expected behavior. (See *Specificity Quiz,* Appendix G.) The chance of the employee guessing the desired behavior is low. I have worked with many supervisors who wanted more initiative, cooperation, or responsibility from their employees. The problem is that these behaviors signify different actions to different people. To one person cooperation means *obedience without question.* To another it means *checking to make sure they got the information accurately before proceeding.* To still another it means *disagreeing with instructions that seem error-prone.* Another thinks of cooperation as *being warm and friendly with each other.*

So, reprimands are inevitable and, when stated in general and judgmental ways, are destructive because they are unclear and the corrective action desired is often misunderstood by the employee.

For reprimands to be constructive, the following conditions must exist:

1. Job assignments are clear.

2. Expectations about how those jobs are to be accomplished have been specified.

3. Positive reinforcements are common. People more often hear what they are doing right than what they are doing wrong.

4. There is a climate of openness in the work group. It is okay to differ and okay to paraphrase to see if understanding is being communicated.

5. Reprimands are given:[29]

    a. privately, not publicly
    b. with specific behaviors or actions listed
    c. so the timing is very close to the event

---

[29] Ken Blanchard, in his book, *The One-Minute Manager,* illustrates these in a similar way.

d. with a pause after the reprimand, to make sure that future
    action expectations are clear

e. with a reassuring statement after the reprimand, affirming the
    value of this person to you.

Factor 25 ∼ Work Relationships

Action Idea: Constantly Maintain Good Work Relationships

Most conflict at work is not interpersonal. It is inevitable that individuals
will have so-called interpersonal conflicts when there is poor sponsorship,
unclear roles and priorities, and confused authority and decision making.
However, these resulting conflicts cannot be resolved interpersonally
because the root cause lies elsewhere. Not understanding this, most people relieve their stress by gossiping. Talking *about* someone instead of *to*
someone is so familiar that it seems part of the natural order of things —
"the way it is."

There are both positive and negative aspects of gossiping, of *talking about,*
someone else. It is positive, for example, when we simply relay information between others. Also, the positive effects are easy to list when it is
you who is upset with someone else. Talking with a confidant about
another person helps you to:

- let off steam

- get mutual support (usually)

- gain emotional strength

- be able to survive the next encounter.

But how about when someone else is upset with you, and they talk about it
to someone else, not to you? Suppose they talk to others about your work
behavior, and further, suppose half of the things they mention are opinions
that do not fit your view of yourself or the actual circumstances? The other
person may feel better by blowing off steam and be better able to cope, but
where does that leave you? When you do not get the information you need

while others are getting it through gossip about you, the possibility of this being destructive to all parties and to productivity is high. This is especially true because the chances are high that the conflict seems interpersonal but probably is supported by the root causes mentioned here in the opening paragraph. However, gossip is so ingrained that it is easy to feel helpless about changing the negative, destructive effects.

A word sometimes used to describe this situation is *triangulation.* Think of it this way:

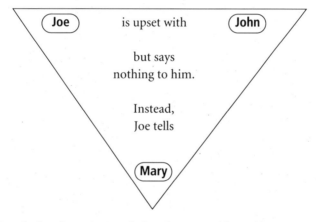

A triangle has been created that has cut John off, and he has no access to information he could use either to change direction or to clear up misunderstandings. (Conversely, *positive* information can also be communicated in this way and be withheld from John, which keeps him from getting reinforcement needed to stay on track.)

So, now what can be done? Joe and Mary can actually use this situation to gain positive results. They can make agreements from among the following alternatives:

1. Joe will talk it through with Mary to see if this upset really has anything to do with John. He may discover that it has little to do with John. Perhaps it has to do with root causes mentioned earlier (which should be addressed) or with behavior on *Joe's* part that he now realizes is typical and dysfunctional for him.

2. Joe may discover that John did do some specific things that Joe can describe that upset him and/or affected work. In that case, Mary may assist Joe in planning how he will handle this with John. In addition, Mary can also help Joe discuss the benefits and costs of talking to John. By *no* means should people always be direct! The risks should be assessed.

3. Joe may ask Mary to be a third party (a facilitator) to a conversation between him and John. Maybe she is a friend of both or respected by both and her presence could help each listen and talk more clearly. *She would not go as a judge or arbitrator as to who is right or wrong.*

4. Mary may suggest a neutral person who could be a third party to the conversation. Some companies have trained staff available to do this.

Being in a role like Mary's puts one in a strong position to turn potential triangulation into positive outcome. In this example it is important that Mary do one of the above alternatives to produce a positive outcome. It is Joe's problem to solve. Otherwise, by simply continuing to listen, Mary is helping to make the problem worse; if she persists in listening over and over again to the same gripes, she is contributing to the problem. If this is the case, Mary should examine what she has to gain from keeping the problem unsolved. If Joe refuses to talk to John, Mary must stop the conversations. It is difficult to do this and still stay connected. Mary needs to say, "Joe, I want to stay a friend, but I won't talk about John anymore."

When the Joes and Marys of organizations handle triangulation as recommended here, the result will be better communication, and problems will get resolved instead of entrenched. Higher morale and benefits to productivity, quality, and safety will likely follow. Of course, if the information is critical to the organization's work, Mary may choose to tell Joe that she cannot keep this a secret. Telling this to Joe becomes a fifth alternative. Secrets are more devastating to organizations than truth.

Chapter Four

Focus on System Change, Not Individual Change

During the 1960s, pop psychology entered the cultural mainstream of the United States. Such books as Thomas Harris' best seller, *I'm OK, You're OK,* (1969) made it okay to talk about feelings and relationships. Personal encounter groups blossomed from Berkeley to Boston to Biloxi. On into the 70s, organizations from Mind Dynamics to LifeSpring to EST turned personal growth into a thriving industry. Biofeedback devices let people tune in electronically and tune their brain waves toward the alpha state — the best legal high of them all. It became more acceptable to have a therapist, and amateur psychologists at every cocktail party issued snap judgments about the nature of your particular hang-up. The personality era was "in."

Two decades later, many who were influenced by that era have traded their peace buttons and jeans for suits and briefcases and become managers. Enhanced by the movement, many retain a "psyching out" habit — the use of simplistic, pop-psychology terms to describe complex human behavior — thereby often missing the powerful way that organizations and groups affect individual behavior.

The psyching out habit is practiced by those who label as "deviants" and "troublemakers" those with whom they have conflict on the job. Terms like "he's a loser," "she's turf-hungry," or "he's egocentric," elicit nods of approval from others who hear such phrases as *real talk* or talk that is *telling it like it is.* When persons have been so labeled, the impulse of many is to lose the distinction between judgments and facts and thereby assume that the issue is rooted in a "personality problem" existing, of course, in the other party. The simplistic solution is to train, transfer, or fire the problem person.

The Powerful But Forgotten Performance Formula

Some sixty years ago Kurt Lewin, known as the "practical theorist," offered a simple but profound formula that if comprehended and practiced, would save managers much frustration and organizations millions of dollars misspent on individually-focused training. Lewin's brief and insightful formula is:

$$Behavior = f(Person \ x \ Environment)$$

Behavior is a function of the person times the environment.

It is a simple formula whose true meaning is seldom understood or applied. To understand how it works, consider the example of Pat, an average employee. Every organization has plenty of Pats. Pats perform okay work, not exceptional but good enough to get by. From time to time they blow off steam, complaining about the potholes in the parking lot, the temperature in the back room, the equipment that keeps breaking down, or that management doesn't seem to care.

Co-workers shrug it off with, "Oh, you know Pat." But Pat's well-meaning supervisor, having just returned from a management seminar that emphasized individual motivation, concludes that Pat's behavior reflects an underlying attitude problem and rewrites Lewin's formula to become:

$$Behavior = f(Person)$$

Behavior is the function of the individual's personal traits.

When Pat is diagnosed by the manager as having a personality problem, possible solutions appear obvious — communication training, counseling, lectures on cooperation, reprimand, or ignore the problem and hope that it will go away. But these solutions make the fundamental assumption that change in systems comes solely from changes in individuals. Is this so?

"No!" said Lewin. But in the 20th century psychological culture, the *individual* personality problem concept grabs most of us as powerfully as the flat-earth concept once did. In earlier centuries the *demon in people* myth or concept, held as fact, led to the death of thousands of women. They were called *witches* — and that name-calling was held as a reality, not an opinion.

Likewise, using a viewpoint based on popular psychological concepts is one way of viewing the world, but it is not the final reality. Many in the 20th century are stuck in that psychological paradigm or myth — more stuck than they comprehend.

This brings us to an important principle for the manager in quest of excellence:

Focus on *system* change rather than individual *personality* change.

If managers keep thinking that boosting organizational performance is solely a matter of individual personality, they will continue to try to correct organizational ills through individually-focused approaches, as if system-wide problems can be corrected by whipping individuals into shape with the latest motivational cassette series.

Most of the problems stifling organizations are systemic. That is, they are influenced by patterns that have become normative in the culture of that group or organization. In one firm three percent of the staff were chronically late for work. Management decided to solve the problem by firing those chronic latecomers. But six months later the company again had three percent of its staff show up late, even though the original latecomers were no longer there. Why the continuing tardiness? The tardiness occurred because the organization functioned in a way that continued to create three percent chronic latecomers; its basic system encouraged new people to take on certain dysfunctional roles. It was run by an authoritarian boss who tried to be a nice guy, was not clear with employees about the consequences of unacceptable behavior, but came down with a heavy hand at an unexpected moment on unsuspecting employees. Sudden punishment without warning is inevitable in authoritarian systems.

When organizations begin to think systemically, they no longer primarily focus on trying to change the individual. Instead, they seek to discover and correct the underlying issue(s) causing that system to create undesirable behavior. In the case of the chronic late comers, perhaps the employees were overloaded from spending inordinate effort accounting for time and expenditures, inefficiency from poor work-flow patterns, too much noise, poor supervisory coordination and prioritization, or from being expected to do things that conflicted with organizational policy. These are systems issues, as are potentially all 25 of the High Performance Factors.

As long as such issues are not addressed, employees will inevitably manifest hostility. This hostility is expressed when employees sabotage the equipment or steal tableware from the company cafeteria to outfit their summer cabin. Or the hostility may be covert, when people work *just enough* not to get reprimanded or consistently come to work late. Whatever the form of hostility, the solution most often is to focus change on the system, which perhaps means helping the boss to be a clear leader. Only when the system is healthy can one begin to identify individuals who are not functioning well because of individual traits rather than faulty organizational systems. (An indicator of system health is high scores on the 25 Factors.) Indeed, there are people who are dysfunctional. Certainly a key theme of this book is that the leader needs to be more differentiated, that is, to be her/his own self and to know what she/he wants, needs, expects, feels, and thinks as a unique self. To be differentiated *and* connected is being touted here as a healthy state. So, what the individual brings to the situation is important. Lewin's theory helps define what I believe to be an appropriate balance between the individual and the system.

However, popular street psychology quickly labels Pat, from our earlier example, as having a personality problem. These *street-psychological* terms popularly used are very unsophisticated. Professional psychologists can well object to our even calling it psychological language. But any language that is an interpretation of another person (he is a complainer, dominator, or controller; she is irresponsible, childish, or aggressive) is in the *individual personality* paradigm. *Pat is none of these!* Pat is Pat, and Pat just happens to do certain things that some people interpret one way and others interpret differently.

The eye of the beholder sees Pat's behavior in a certain way and the mind of the beholder fixes a particular label on that behavior. *The labels people use to describe others tell us more about the person who is speaking than about the person being described.*

We can find other observers of Pat who see the same behavior but call it by a different name. Mary may label Pat's behavior as "playful," while John labels the same actions "aggressive." Pat may be viewed as "full of good ideas" by some while others in that same meeting may call Pat "domineering." That different people can reach such different conclusions about the same behavior should warn us about the danger of taking our labels too seriously and about the danger of focusing on the problem as being individual rather than systemic. Of course we judge, interpret, and label others. And that is okay, as long as we realize the limitations of our labels — they are *our* reality but rarely one shared by the accused. In fact, the accused knows his/her good intentions and has a self-concept based on those intentions. The accuser bases his/her view of the other person's behavior on judgments that are likely to be radically different from what the accused person intended.

I once observed a meeting where a group of engineers presented their female boss with a set of recommendations they had developed for improving the effectiveness of the work group. The group was surprised that she accepted nearly all of the recommendations. Surprise was evident because that boss had been seen as *hopeless* — not redeemable, as impossible to change. Many commented positively about the responsiveness of the boss. However, one employee was very distraught and asked to see me. The conversation went this way:

> *Employee:* "I'm thinking of resigning after what happened at the meeting. She lied and humiliated me in front of the whole group!"
>
> *Crosby:* (Stunned) "What happened?"
>
> *Employee:* "She humiliated me!"

Crosby: "When did she do that? What did she say or do?"

Employee: "Well, you heard her lie!"

When pressed, the employee recounted the incident. Two fellow engineers who were present could not remember the incident and were surprised that this employee felt humiliated. They too had disliked the boss. But, try as they might, they could not comprehend his experience because their experience was so different.

By now the statement, which he had experienced as *humiliation* and labeled a lie, was remembered differently by various persons depending on *their judgments!* For him to see it not as *what happened* — a reality for all — but as his private experience and interpretation was a difficult task. The label he chose for his boss was that she was a liar. To him this was evidenced by *what happened,* but his interpretation of what happened was invisible to all in the room but him.

Later he told other people that she *lied,* and some swallowed this label as if it were reality and as if they had missed something. Undifferentiated as most people are about such common miscommunication, the other engineers did not gather data to clear up the misunderstanding. In short, the employee's reality (perception) would become their reality (perception), especially because they disliked the boss to begin with. They became fused with their friend. They did not step back to see what was happening and maintain their own separate perspective.

Liar. That was the label he chose. A liar distorts communication. The implication is that this was a deliberate act. Who was really the liar? The accuser, the accused, or both? The incident illustrates that the labels chosen are projections onto the accused. Like a movie, those projections were created in his growing-up process long before they were projected onto the *screen* of the accused person. You see behavior(s). You create labels. It is important to know the difference.

We All Interpret Differently

A most critical insight for any manager is to realize that *all judgments about another individual are interpretations of reality rather than reality itself.* That does not mean that such interpretations should not be respected. Interpretive words about Pat are to be respected, but none of those words are the reality. They are simply interpretations, and we each interpret differently.

Your Interpretations Are Just That — Interpretations

For some people the distinction between observable facts and making interpretations may seem like a great deal of nitpicking. For me it is one of the most profound concepts in human communication. Some may think we are saying that you should not judge. We are not. Interpretations exist; they are part of the warp and woof of life. They are to be honored, valued, and often trusted as guides for behavior. But, they are not to be confused with facts.

My interpretations are mine, they come out of my history and life experience. And they will likely not at all be an interpretation that another observer might have at that moment. Even if they had the same interpretation, that would not make it a fact, it would still be an interpretation. Avoid black-and-white thinking here. Simply because I cannot know if my interpretations or evaluations are true does not make them useless. They still help me to make sense out of my situation. The dilemma is that many confuse making sense with the need to have the final answer or unchallengeable fact. Many let their judgmental, interpretive word become the reality.

The ability to distinguish between interpretation and fact is a profound skill in communication. Once we learn this we will honor our interpretations and judgments but not confuse them as if they were a fact about someone or something else. (Much of the failure both in performance appraisal and report writing comes from the inability to make this distinction.)

While human judgment is always involved, conflict can be greatly minimized by translating our interpretations into observable behavior. Behind all judgments lie observable facts. It is ours to choose whether we approach others with our judgments about them, provide them with specifics, or do both.

I have spent much effort working with engineers and other technical specialists who did not understand this distinction. In writing a so-called factual paper they would intersperse judgments/opinions/interpretations, which of course led to misunderstandings and conflicts with those reacting to these so-called *facts*.

The Most Difficult of All Human Skills

To the reader it may seem that what I have been discussing is a simple skill. After reading this far, many could take the *Specificity Quiz* found in Appendix G and score 100%. Looks are deceiving. As an academic exercise it is simple. In the crunch it is lost on almost everyone.

To survive our brain forms rapid judgments. In moments of anxiety, threat, and fear these rapid judgments overpower rational thinking. In that crisis moment, judgment/interpretations and facts become as if they were one. For our ancestors this was important for survival. They reacted quickly to danger; they fought or fled. However, such reactivity (an undifferentiated state) is disastrous in a modern work setting or a personal relationship.

Then how can we learn to use this skill in those tough moments? Put simply, those projections were deeply learned at ages one day to five years. When people defend quickly with projections/interpretations that they are *sure are the truth*, you are dealing with basic, gut-level stuff.

All of us have a touch, usually a strong touch, of such unresolved, early trigger reactions. Differentiated training and effective counseling can help us make these distinctions. Sharp managers who would follow the suggestions given in this book will look to a trusted, clear, differentiated friend or a therapist for growth in this area.

Those who tend to confuse interpretations (labels) with facts also tend to think that individual behavior is a personality/motivation issue. They would also change Kurt Lewin's theory to: *Behavior = f(Person)*.

The Limitations of Training

Business and industry have created enormous training programs on models of desirable, individual behavior. In technical fields this can be appropriate, but in people-related areas individually-focused training has a poor track record. Ironically, the true intent of training is best achieved when individual training is undertaken in the context of a systems approach to organizational vitality. The notion that organizational change can come from individualized emphasis is very alive and well! But B=f(P) is dysfunctional. Taking individuals out of the work setting, training them, then sending them back often does not work, especially in human relations skills like supervision.

Recall attending a management training session that was stimulating and exciting, where you took lengthy notes and looked forward to making changes in your work when you returned. But back on the job, plop. Nothing happened. You tried, but you could not translate those wonderful concepts into action. The problem was not with the concepts you learned; you no doubt improved your management style. The underlying cause of whatever performance problems there were was not just in your management style but in the larger system. It usually does not work to focus primarily on individual change unless there is change in the system in which that individual operates. New, *state-of-the-art* packaged training programs are often more of the same — money poured down the drain on an *individual* approach. Training is important, but the benefits are greatly enhanced when the sponsor includes the training as an integral part of a strategy to achieve organizational values and business objectives *and* has a systems perspective.

Skewing the Equation the Other Way

Now, the other extreme would be to have the theory read:

$$B=f(E).$$

Behavior is a function of the environment.

That would imply that all workable solutions come from systems and structural thinking alone. If we change the environment, we change all people. That would also be an unbalanced notion. So, the beautiful balance of Kurt Lewin's theory remains — $B=f(PxE)$. Both the person *and* the environment are vitally involved in the kind of work place behavior that promotes excellence.

Notice that Lewin put a *multiplier* sign, not a *plus* sign, between the (P) and (E). Each person (P) in the equation is a unique creature who brings his or her own history to work, complete with individual abilities, characteristics, and quirks. Then, individualness is *multiplied* by the environment (E). If the environment is one where mistrust is rampant, then whatever personal experience people have with mistrust will be multiplied and they will continually protect their flanks while suspecting everyone and everything. If the organization is one of high trust, then people's experience with mistrust will be minimized; their history with trusting situations will be multiplied, and they will operate more openly and non-defensively.

The significant part of Lewin's equation is the interaction of person and environment. We have all witnessed the proverbial square peg in the round hole, the person who, ineffective and unmotivated where he was, became a splendid performer when moved to another department. It was not the person who changed. The improved performance came about because the climate and conditions of his new job environment were different.

Back to our engineer who labeled his boss as a liar. What he brings to this situation is great distrust flamed by an important history related to the word *liar*. Private work with him revealed a strong moralism about *lying* and a life history of labeling many people as liars. (It was his most used judgmental word.) Minimal insights by him into his style was important before system steps would work. In subsequent weeks we worked out the following conditions:

1. Clear agreements between the employees and the boss. This included a clear statement (specific, not general) from the boss about what she expected.

2. A special agreement *not* to triangulate, that is, not to talk about each other negatively to others (except to get help in planning for a subsequent conversation). (See Factor 25, *Constantly Maintain Good Work Relationships.*)

3. More consistent contact between the employees and the boss.

4. Improvement in departmental role clarity, evaluation processes, and delegation of authority by the boss. All three areas had been identified in earlier data gathering and had contributed to conflict between the boss and employees.

5. Clear follow-through with a third party present initially, and then an expanded follow-through to include problem solving and information giving on a regular weekly basis without the third party present.

I did not focus on the one *troubled* employee but on the group and the boss. Key new behaviors for the boss were to (1) state her expectations, (2) have increased casual contact with the employees, and (3) follow through. While these might be seen as expected boss behaviors, I find that most bosses have difficulty with all three.

Not focusing on the so-called *troubled* employee was a deliberate strategy. He had manifested great difficulty in being rational. He was not differentiating. Whereas other workers could agree or disagree with the boss (e.g., "I like that idea" or "I'm concerned about that expectation"), his language was blaming and was about the boss ("You're a liar"). Or it was general ("*You* always do that" or "*We* all think you are lying"). This person drained the energy of the boss or group with his lack of clarity and apparent inability to speak in "I" language. While others would occasionally blame or use victim-language ("It's not my fault" or "They made us do it"), they would usually speak for themselves and could engage in rational problem solving.

This case highlights a major difference between clear, differentiated behavior and reactive, undifferentiated behavior. The engineer in question was so caught up in his emotional field that his constant resistance would not have been more obvious had he worn a suit of armor. His intensity was so great that he had lost his capacity, for example, to be specific. Even if he could score well on the *Specificity Quiz* referenced here in Appendix G, he had lost the capacity to use that skill or think that way in this conflict. It is unproductive and demoralizing for the boss to spend *group* time focusing on such a member. However, it is not unusual for bosses to give undue attention to the most difficult, recalcitrant individual. This signals that the boss is hooked by or captured by that person. Sometimes a boss will say that the other person "pushed my button." But such language is undifferentiated victim talk. *I push my own buttons.* Others do what *they* do, but they do not control my emotions — I do — and it is a cop-out to say otherwise.

Individually this person was highly skilled technically. Therefore, with the sabotage (triangulating) monitored and curtailed, the boss continued to employ him. The boss' ability to be clear about herself and what she wanted was a key factor. She did not become reactive in response to his reactive, emotional behavior. Also, she did not abdicate leadership or give up her authority. She initiated new patterns of interaction. She agreed to delegate in areas where the workers clearly had expertise, and she initiated friendly hello's, whereas in the past she had been seen as quite distant and was judged as a *snob*. It will not surprise most readers to know that she had previously kept her distance because she felt unsure of herself and unclear about how to balance her own authority with employee influence.

No matter how healthy the system, there will be difficult employees. But effective leaders do not waste time on recalcitrants. If resistance is handled as stated above (also reread the sections on *Openness* and *Reprimands),* the resistance is likely to lessen. Difficult employees need one-on-one clarity, where a boss makes clear specifically what is expected and what will and will not be tolerated. Given such behavioral clarity, they then should be offered a clear choice about whether to stay or leave.

I have found that when a boss is clear about behavioral expectations, as referenced in the Reprimand Action Ideas beginning on page 70, a high majority of so-called troubled employees begin to function well. Whether the change is impacted most by the new clarity, the resulting healthier system, or the realization that one's job is on the line, is not known. Probably all three are important.

Here is another example. The boss sets the context for a meeting with a perceived-to-be difficult employee by telling the employee that he/she (the boss) wants him (the employee) to succeed. She points out that this is not now the case and that it will take certain, specific behaviors to turn around the unsatisfactory behavior and put him on a road to success.

Beyond being clear, the boss should not explain or defend her position. It is effective for her to ask, "Do you need something from me to help you achieve these expectations?" However, remember that this is not a time of shared agreement. This is a moment when *a boss is a boss is a boss.* She plans a follow-through with this employee in two weeks and again in four weeks. The pattern will be clear by then. If the results are negative, she will act. A leader's primary function is to be clear about expectations, encourage success, provide support, give specific feedback, and then reward or if necessary bite the bullet and reprimand, which can include dismissal. Of course, all of this is a pattern of boss behavior that creates a high performance system. Such a boss is differentiated and connected. And such behaviors manifest that elusive balance between management authority and employee influence.

Distinguishing Between the Approaches

To contrast an individual approach with a systems approach, consider how you would respond to the scenarios that follow.

Scenario I

One of your computer analysts comes to you. He appears sad and depressed, with head hanging and eyes aimed on the ground. What do you do?

> **Option A:** You explore his feelings and try to uncover any recent problems he has had — is he having marriage woes or financial difficulties? Or you give him some advice — check in to the Health Clinic, take the rest of the day off, or get off his duff and get back to work.

> **Option B:** You ask what is going well and what is not going well at work. You pursue how clear this person is about his role and whether he has the information and authority to do his work. You find out if his opinions are sought when decisions are made that will affect his work procedures or the equipment and materials he uses. You examine how clear you have been about your sponsorship.

Notice that the Option A response to the problem is *individual* and *personal*. The advice has to do with what the worker can do to recover. This option assumes an individual problem.

Option B is the *systems* option. Management processes have to be shifted to change the *environment* or some part of the environment (e.g., role clarity, clarity about who is boss, etc.). If all of the items listed in Option B are in place and the depression persists, then the Option A response may be appropriate.

Scenario II

Several mechanics have complained to you about the storeroom manager who reports to you. She seems to forget where things are or, at least, cannot find them. The mechanics must sometimes wait an hour for the parts they need. At other times they check to see if some out-of-stock parts they requested two weeks earlier have arrived and they find the order was not placed, which holds up maintenance for two more weeks until parts arrive. What do you do?

> **Option A:** You suggest that the storeroom manager attend a workshop on time or stress management. You suggest a new computerized program for recording inventory.

> **Option B:** You examine your clarity as her leader. Have you described your expectations clearly? (No generalizations, such as be cooperative, show initiative, etc.) Have you sponsored well? (See Factor 1.) Does she have the authority to do what she is expected to do? (See Factor 14.) Have you talked about her to others instead of to her? (See Factor 25.) How does maintenance contribute to the problem? Are there clear procedures?

Option A is the *individual* approach. "If that individual would only approach the situation or her life differently, the problem would be solved." Option B is more *systemic*. It defines your part in the *dance*. It assumes that the problem lies primarily in the systems surrounding the storeroom manager before dealing with her as if the problem were an individual one.

Scenario III

A peer approaches you about an oft-repeated gripe she has about her boss. You are a first-line supervisor, as is she. What do you do?

> **Option A:** You listen to her story and sympathize.

> **Option B:** You say that you cannot give her advice except to suggest that she go directly to her boss rather than talk with you about it. And because you have a good relationship with her boss, you say further that you would be glad to go in with her.

Option A, the *individual* option, assumes that listening to her story will help. It may be that the listening (too much) is part of the (informal) system that is contributing to the problem. Note that Option B sets up a way to handle the conflict.

Family therapists refer to triangulation. When you come to me about your problems with another person, I triangulate if I become your outlet. If I listen in order to help you think through your approach to the other person and suggest you go there, go with you, or help you find a skilled neutral facilitator, then I am not triangulating. Major transformations are created by the agreement and successful practice of *not* triangulating in groups and organizations. (See Factor 25, *Constantly Maintain Good Work Relationships.*)

Scenario IV

You work in a small business and your boss is a son of the owner. On recent occasions when the owner had lunch with you, he hinted that he was unhappy with his son's management and was thinking of replacing him with you. You do not think that would work and do not want to see that happen, even though it would provide you with a personal gain. The owner has just called you about having lunch tomorrow, and you suspect the purpose is to discuss plans to replace his son with you. What to do?

> **Option A:** You think through the situation and mentally rehearse exactly what you will say to the owner. You may even seek advice about how to proceed when you meet the owner. You jot down the key points you want to make and practice your opening lines.

> **Option B:** You call the owner and tell him you cannot make lunch and that you think it is important for the success of the business that the two of you not meet further until the owner talks directly with his son about his dissatisfaction with his son's management.

Option A, the *individual* option, is more of the same. The words matter little — what is significant is that you are meeting. Option B creates a radical (root) shift that highlights the issue. You are at risk with either alternative. Option B could imply that you do not want that job. You risk your relationship with the owner. Obviously, if you do not want to assume that particular risk, you will choose Option A. Recognize that by the very fact of meeting, you may continue your close association with the owner and leave the son on the outside. Consider this: if the owner treats his son this way what might you guess will be the owner's behavior if he becomes dissatisfied with you?

Scenario V

Among the mechanics in your shop, it is very clear that Mike, a new worker, is seen as being a problem. Dealing with Mike presents you with the following possibilities:

> **Option A:** Bring Mike in for a talk and make it clear what Mike must and must not do for his work to be considered satisfactory. Initiate some disciplinary procedures, so he gets the message that you mean business.

> **Option B:** Meet with the group to find out what is and is not going well. Specifically, explore whether people get the information and materials they need to do a good job and whether they have the authority they need. Find out how clear they are about their tasks and priorities and if they are able to influence the purchase of equipment they maintain. Also, notice how they engage in conversation. Do many talk or just a couple people? Do they interact with you or just react?

Interpreting Your Responses

By now it should be clear that Option B in all cases is more systemic. Also, my bias is to go the route of Option B before attempting Option A. Notice not just the words of people and groups but the pattern of the interaction. For example, in Scenario V if only a few people talk and they are primarily reactive to you, then Mike may have joined a negative system and could be being made the scapegoat.

Choosing individual strategies may get results today and satisfy your reactive need, but if the system does not change and you do not dance differently, then the same problems will surface again and again. Also, you may be caught up in the 20th century individual culture. If so, it is highly unlikely that your efforts to boost productivity, quality, and morale, and to reduce stress will achieve the level of success you desire.

Role Confusion: A Typical Systems Issue

Our surveys of thousands of American workers across numerous industries show a surprising lack of clarity concerning roles and responsibilities. The statement, "People around here seem to be clear about what their job is," produced the following results on the *People Performance Profile*: (6 is high with "Almost Always" to "Almost Never" as possible extreme responses):

Senior Management	2.69
Middle Management	2.27
Hourly Workers	2.64

In one organization we studied, confusion over roles ran rampant across the whole system. The data revealed not only that hourly employees were unclear about what was expected of them but so were middle and top managers. In the worst tradition of individual focus and blame, people were living under stress and constantly being accused of not doing their jobs. Appeals would be made for individual excellence and, of course, the response was defensiveness. Bosses were accused of not caring and of being disorganized.

The CEO and the other three top executives were clear about their jobs. Therefore they dismissed questions about role clarity as irrelevant. However, when it became clear from the data and from the reports that role clarity and prioritization were system-wide issues, the top executives began to address their roles with the people immediately under them, who in turn did so at the next level and so on throughout the company (see Factor 12, *Clarify Roles/Jobs*).

System-wide issues can be addressed to some degree in organization sub-units (such as work teams), but they will never be resolved fully until addressed from the very top of the company. Role clarification, if that is a system-wide issue, must begin with senior management or at the very apex of the organization if indeed the chief executive lives in a fog of unclarity.

The quest for organizational excellence must address all three levels: individual, group, and organizational. Many perceived individual problems will vanish if the leader embraces the principles and pursues the implementation strategies recommended in this book. Not all individual problems will disappear, of course, but what we now think of as individual personality issues will be greatly reduced.

All improvement efforts need to be examined to see if they rest on the false notion that more individual effort or individual change is the road to organizational strength. In a world of systems thinking in technical approaches, we must also shift to systems thinking about human resources. Once that shift is clearly in place, we will have kicked the *fix-the-individual-only habit*. Instead, we will create strategies that work on the optimum interconnection of the individual and the environment.

Chapter Five

Survey Feedback — Turning Data Into Action

We know what does *not* work. It does not work to survey people and not show them the results. It also does not work to survey people and have top management or an outside expert develop recommendations (prescriptions). It does not work to survey people and have a general session and report the results to all concerned and do nothing else. These approaches all have been tried hundreds of times and, with rare exception, been found wanting. People become irritable and defensive, with a resulting lowered morale and decreased work efficiency.

What Does Work?

Begin with the assumption that the expertise to identify problems and *work out solutions* to most problems *exists within the organization.* The suggestions that follow encourage you to involve the participants in generating the data, interpreting that data, and forging recommendations for next steps. This assumes that people in your organization have expertise and knowledge and that the job of management is to tap that vein of experience. The late Dr. Ronald Lippitt spoke of a *fundamental right:* "They who put their pencil to the survey paper should also see and work the data" (from a private conversation with John Scherer and Robert Crosby).

Dr. Fred Fosmire, former vice president of Organizational and Employee Relations at Weyerhaueser, writes: "Survey feedback methods, when implemented competently by managers who are receptive to feedback, may be the most powerful way we know to improve organization effectiveness."

Positive involvement is vital to organizational effectiveness. There is no more effective way than survey feedback (turning data into action) to involve people quickly at the key points of data gathering, problem solving, solution recommending, action, and follow-through.

Doing Survey Feedback with Your Employees

Survey feedback, *well done,* will increase morale, improve work processes, heal broken work relationships, shift culture, and put into action effective, high-performing behaviors more quickly than any other intervention. (See Display One, Appendix K, for examples of shifts in cultural behaviors and attitudes.)

I have spawned survey feedback activities in over 500 organizations and have facilitated hundreds of groups from top management to unionized laborers. Here is an overview of the characteristics of a *well-done* survey feedback process. Specific steps and "how-to's" follow.

1. A well-done survey feedback process is solidly sponsored.

2. Participants are carefully oriented as to the purpose and the steps of survey feedback, including dates.

3. Questions are answered anonymously.

4. Data is fed back to the work group that generated the data, with no interpretation.

5. The time lapse between doing the survey and receiving the data is less than two weeks.

6. The sessions are led by a skilled facilitator. (He/she could be the manager. See Appendix J, *Characteristics of an Effective Facilitator.*) This facilitator is one who can handle conflict directly, can remain

neutral about outcomes, is adept at guiding a problem-solving process without being derailed by resistant members (or sponsors), and knows well the skill illustrated in the *Specificity Quiz* (see Appendix G).

7. As the people work the data, they illustrate both strengths and issues, with specificity rather than generally, and work in a context of "make it happen" rather than "find fault and blame."

8. Specific agreements are developed. No general, interpretative language (words like adequate, better, etc.) is permissible. Employees are encouraged to create their own new ways to solve problems as well as to ask for what they need from the boss and other groups.

9. A clear decision is made by the sponsor about her/his part of any agreement.

10. Follow-through is scheduled when enough time has passed to live out the agreements. (No longer than three weeks.)

11. Follow-through continues and becomes integrated into staff meetings, with problem-solving methods applied to new issues again and again.

Beyond the survey feedback process, a next, easy step as agreements are being reached is to develop the team measurements described in Factor 16.

Dimensions of the Survey Feedback Process and Action Steps

Once your sponsorship is in place and an instrument is chosen,[30] there are three key dimensions to the survey feedback work. The first is preparatory. The orientation to the survey feedback steps is an excellent opportunity to

---

[30] You may create your own, use the 25 Factors in this book, or use instruments as referenced on page 19.

be clear about your mission, values, and business objectives. If you have not already shared these, it is critical that you do so now. Give your employees an orientation that models openness. Later we suggest an effective way to do an orientation with your employees. (See *Orientation Session,* Appendix K.)

The second key is the presentation and problem-solving of the data with the people involved and developing recommendations for action. A skilled facilitator is important because this step can invoke intense emotionality, especially if people have felt suppressed prior to this activity. (See *Data Feedback and Problem-Solving Session,* Appendix L.)

The third key dimension is the follow-through. You, the sponsor, control that. This needs to be planned and scheduled up front so that the expectation from the beginning is that follow-through is a norm. Dates should be announced.

Action Steps

1. Have an initial orientation and administration of the survey.

2. Score the data.

3. Feed back the data to the group and have the teams engage in problem solving.

4. Present recommendations to the decision maker (if he/she has not been part of the problem solving) *after* sharing commitments that the team members have made to improve work practices. Hear and discuss decisions by boss(es), including by-whens — dates that the decisions will be implemented. (See Appendix L.)

5. Commence actions.

6. Conduct follow-through sessions in three weeks or less and then at least monthly. (See *Follow-Up Meetings,* Appendix M).

Besides data-gathering, survey feedback is a prime opportunity to initiate second order change.[31] Using survey feedback simply to identify issues or solve problems is to miss the power of using it to *be* and *act* in new ways. Think of recommendations and agreements as change of the first order. But more importantly, while doing survey feedback, you can *put in place* new ways of working to support your mission. That is, by meeting *by-when* commitments and not merely talking about it, by *doing* effective follow-through or *doing* measurements, or by *being* open, your work team behavior will shift in the desired direction. Well-done survey feedback creates a *way of life* — a culture shift — a second order change — that will help you continuously to achieve objectives.

How Does Turning Data Into Action Work in a Large System?

1. Turning data into action begins with the orientation and adminis-tration of a survey or with interviews.

2. It continues with the feeding back of this data to the appropriate work group. For example, if the mechanics have filled out the data, then they get back the mechanics' data.

3. Then, at the same time, the data is used in problem-solving sessions to help each work group plan ways to improve its work practices and develop recommendations to present to its boss. In some orga-nizations the supervisor leads this session. In others the supervisor leaves for a brief time while employees are developing a list of what they need more of or less of from their supervisor in order to func-tion more effectively.[32] Doing this in the context of the survey feed-back with effective guidance helps group members to be specific about their needs.

---

[31] See Watzlawick, Weakland, & Fisch. (1974). *Change.* New York, London: W. W. Norton & Co.

[32] The temporary absence of the boss gives employees an opportunity to gain clarity about what they need from the boss (more of and less of). After initial venting of feelings, they get specific with effective guidance by a skilled leader. Also, it is a chance to prepare a list of those behaviors and qualities appreciated in the organization and in the boss.

4. Next, task forces may meet to do problem solving on systems problems that have emerged. These systems problems are discovered by looking at survey data to see, first, what issues are present across the total organization and, second, what each work group is addressing.

    The systems problems and recommendations are correlated so that those recommendations are made to that total department or unit or plant. Decisions about who gets which recommendations are made at this time. Many go directly to supervisors of smaller units.

5. Everyone who is to receive a recommendation needs briefing and training for that session. For example, the president will be receiving recommendations from the vice presidents, the VPs will be receiving recommendations from staff under them, and so forth.

    The staircase model that follows is recommended here. This process is sponsored by and begins with the president and the vice-president and continues with them for a follow-through period before it commences with the next level. By the time all supervisors or managers receive a recommendation, they presumably will have had a successful experience at giving their recommendations to the management line above them. So, as the process is modelled throughout the organization, sustaining sponsorship is developed, and managers have been coached and have seen a model of how to participate and how to receive and respond to recommendations.

    Prior to receiving requests or recommendations, the manager is told, "You are supposed to help clarify and not argue." And people are told, "You are supposed to be clear and not persuade." Meetings are then held where the recommendations are presented to the appropriate bosses after the employees have shared how they personally intend to improve work practices.

6. Continual coaching is done with supervisors and management regarding their responses to the recommendations. If they do not like a proposed solution, they are invited to inquire about the problem that the solution is intended to address. Solving problems with appropriate input is the goal. Certain solutions (recommendations) may be partial or premature.

7. Sessions are held where the appropriate managers and supervisors meet with their work force to respond to recommendations.

8. A follow-up session is held in two or three weeks and again several weeks later. At these meetings, they look at what has happened, what is working, what is not working, and how they can fix the problems.

Observations

While the eight steps described above occur, all concerned will be alerted to notice certain supervisory problems that need more help than normally would be received by following this typical procedure. There may be special sessions for supervisors on such topics as role clarity, managing and leading more effective meetings, follow-through, developing priorities, performance appraisal, praising, or reprimanding. The agenda for such coaching and training should be clear from data gathered from the surveys and subsequent discussions and observations of how supervisors function during the survey feedback process.

The effective execution of survey feedback creates an important shift in follow-through within many departments where follow-through has been poor. Also, it creates an environment where all members become more clear about the role of top management and about employees' roles in the influence and expertise-sharing processes.

The Staircase Model for Large Organizations

Think of your organization on a staircase that looks like this:

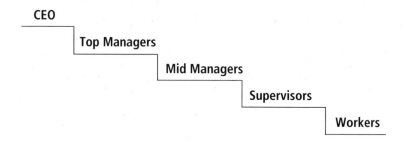

The CEO and Top Managers examine their own survey feedback data and the combined data for the whole organization. Thus, it is the Top Managers who first draft recommendations for the "stair" above them — the CEO.

Top Managers apply problem solving to their data as described, knowing that as the data is worked by the groups down the ladder, there will be mid-course adjustments to meet the newly-identified needs of the other levels' work groups.

Before Mid-Managers present their recommendations to the Top Managers, those Top Managers have already completed that step. The important thing is to have each level far enough along in the process that they will enthusiastically and intelligently sponsor the survey feedback with their employees.

Each stair eventually makes decisions on the recommendations from the stair directly below and reports the decisions back to that stair.

As each stair in your organization experiences these steps, the group's readiness is increased to be supportive in receiving the recommendations from below, until ultimately the entire organization completes this process.

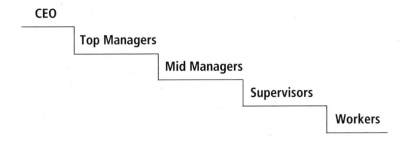

When this work is completed, management behavior shifts will have occurred, reducing the huge black hole of mid-management bureaucracy. In addition, substantive issues will have been dealt with contributing directly to productivity, quality, safety, and other concerns. These recommendations will range from general to specific, but with effective sponsorship and follow-through there will be a fundamental shift in the organization's culture.

Survey feedback is a beginning. For organizations with no prior significant employee involvement, this first step includes "letting off steam." Painful as this is, with skilled, non-defensive leadership the outcomes are exciting and fruitful. Such a process is only for the organization or team whose leader is clear about who he or she is, knows where he/she is headed, and is living in the creative ambiguity of balancing management authority and employee influence. Such a leader is a nonanxious presence in this age of anxiety.

Appendix A

Self-Managing Teams
(or Autonomous Work Teams/Self-Directed Teams)

A Word about Self-Managing Teams

Self-managing teams are becoming popular in the United States and Canada. Patricia Crosby and I have done extensive work in this field at a plant that had the first team-based system in heavy industry in the US. Visitors from other companies are frequent because this plant is known as a model. Also, I have had several recent consultations with major industry managers who are talking the language of self-management.

What Are Self-Managing Teams?

First, "self-managed" means different things to different people (e.g., teams, self-managed teams, participative groups, traditional foreman and workers). Think of it in this way: *A self-managing team manages what it manages and doesn't manage what it doesn't manage.* Sound crazy? Stay with us and consider this example and the following diagram.

Example:

Suppose that a team is expected to manage the following items:

- Safety
- Productivity
- Quality
- Environmental Impact
- Managing Team Meetings Effectively
- Discipline of Tardiness, Absenteeism, and Other Violations.

If there are four teams, will *all* of the teams manage *all* of the items well? Probably not. It is more likely that the time-honored, bell-shaped curve will be in force here as it is in traditionally-managed teams.

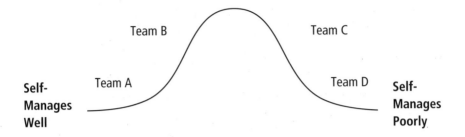

Team B   Team C

Self-   Team A   Team D   **Self-**
Manages   **Manages**
Well   **Poorly**

Even Team A will not manage perfectly. So, who manages what the team is not managing well? This is the question that *must* be addressed. It is the fundamental issue of this book — balancing management authority and employee influence.

Our answer to that question is:

> A supervisor (or equivalent) has single-point accountability and a goal to delegate the managing to the teams. The primary function of the supervisor is to coach and provide training for the team members, so they are able to function like Team A in the bell-shaped curve.

> When the team is not functioning in a high-performing way, the supervisor has single-point accountability to step in and say, "I need this to be handled in _____ hours. If not, I'll manage it."

> Thus, each team defines its degree of self-managing. In essence the challenge is, "You will determine the definition of your self-management by how much you effectively self-manage!"

> After the initial honeymoon period, so-called self-management is very difficult. The larger the group, the more difficult it is. Many such teams look more like *group tyrannies* than the honeymoon dreams of group self-management. *Without clarity about authority and continuous maintenance of work role relationships,* the teams will fail no matter what they are called.

Above all, "self-managed teams" is a method, not an end. The end is to achieve the organization's mission, values, and business objectives. The end is not to create *teams* however defined. Whether there are self-managed teams or more traditional foreman/worker groups, what is critical are the principles we have set forth here. There is no escaping the need for clarity about authority and influence.

In real life we self-manage ourselves within a framework of law and of societal and organizational expectations. Likewise, teams are *created* by some authority and therefore can be disbanded by that same authority. If organizations are to flourish, they must quit pretending about the reality of and need for authority. Authority is not bad or good — it simply is. It can be used for good or ill. Pretending that it does not exist is the kiss of death. Sharing it, with balance, is empowering.

Appendix B

Three States of
Group and Organizational Systems[33]

I — Undifferentiated Fusion

When people are not Selves and do not own their internal experience, you cannot tell who is who . . .

. . . and you will find no learning, high dependence, victims, perpetrators, and rescuers

II — Differentiated Clarity

When people are Selves, disclose their internal experience, and inquire about others' experiences, you can tell where one begins and the other leaves off and . . .

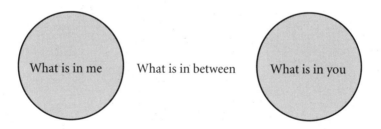

. . . you will find learners, greater clarity, accountability, and personal responsibility.

---

[33] From *A Special Kind of Leadership: The Key to Creating Learning Organizations,* by Ronald R. Short, The Leadership Group, 1990, Seattle, WA.

III — Differentiated Creativity

And this just may lead to . . .

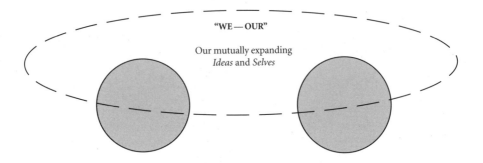

"WE — OUR"

*Our mutually expanding
Ideas and Selves*

. . . more than you dreamed possible.

I — The Undifferentiated Fusion State

Motive: Create safety — protect.

*"**If** they (he, she) would . . .*

*"**If** . . .*

*. . . **then,** and only then, I could . . ."*

*"**If** they (he, she) would . . .*

*. . . **then,** and only then, I could . . . "*

*. . . **then,** and only then, I could . . . "*

*"**If** they (he, she) would . . ."*

Result: Confusion, helplessness, victim(s), perpetrator(s), rescuer(s).

Definition: May appear to be very separate (e.g., "in's, out's," factions, cliques, "we vs. they") but is fused because:

Group A (and/or person A) needs **B** to feel, think, or want something different so *A can feel better about Self*.

Group B (and/or person B) needs **A** to feel, think, or want something different so *B can feel better about Self*.

Neither B nor A are *responsible for* and *in charge of* their own internal experience. Each is dependent upon the other.

Indicators: Individuals are anxiety- and fear-driven *and* this is not talked about.

All acts can become political, i.e., behavior is interpreted and done for intended impact.

"Hi, good morning . . ." 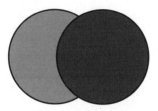 "hmm . . . she obviously wants me to . . .'

There is little inquiry for information to understand the real problem.

Information is selectively shared; both what is shared and with whom.

Secrets are common, the norm.

Effort is put into managing the image and perceptions, not the problem.

How problems are solved *is* the problem . . . *"Well, I'm gonna command 'em to initiate."*

Attempts to solve problems foster and fester new problems.

Work is hard to go to in the morning. *". . . Sigh . . . Another day . . ."*

Transition: Using Your Self — Becoming a Differentiated Leader

Motive: Take risks, learn, act for the good of self and organization.

Result: Just may create movement toward health (no guarantees).

Definition: The differentiated leader is a more transparent Self, taking risks with appropriate people. Understands and acknowledges his or her internal motives, feelings, and thoughts. The leader:

- has vision; sets direction
- expects resistance
- stays true to his or her vision, Self, and role
- remains open to influence
- stays in contact with Self and others
- uses mutual inquiry to learn from his or her experience with people
- acts in the midst of confusion
- is open to being wrong; learns and self-corrects.

Indicators: Leader is clear, less dependent.

Sabotage; resistance.

Tension; pressure; people "for" and "against" direction.

Gradual shift to more openness, clarity.

Communication becomes clearer, more trusted.

Work may be a little scary to go to in the morning.

II — The Differentiated Clarity State

Motive: Clarity, learning, action.

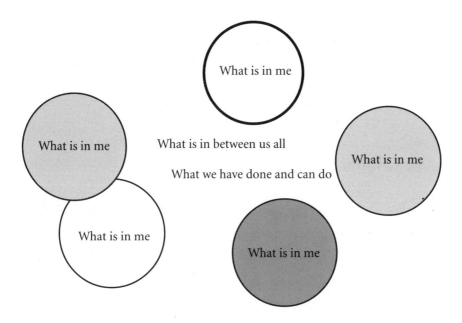

Result: Increased trust, communication, individual responsibility.

Definition: At times may appear to be negative, just contentious (e.g., argument, disagreement, conflict) but is not, because:

Group A (or person A) learns the feelings, thoughts, and motives of B

Group B (or person B) learns the feelings, thoughts, and motives of B

Both know the other knows

Neither is dependent upon what the other feels, thinks, or wants in order to feel good about himself/herself.

Indicators: Clear boundaries between feedback and formal, organizational evaluation.

Problem solving.

Clarity about the internal states of people. Declarative statements common.

Mutual inquiry.

Ownership; personal involvement.

Respect and acknowledgement of differences.

Descriptive rather than judgmental.

Going to work is sometimes painful . . . but empowering.

III — The Differentiated Creativity State

Motive: Quality, productivity, creative expansion of ideas and people.

Result: Quality, cohesion, creative ideas, community, productivity.

Definition: A new kind of fusion that comes from acknowledged, individual differences. People are pulled, not pushed, into the

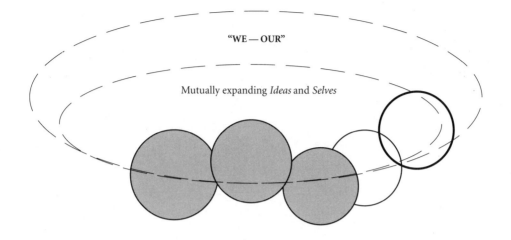

"WE — OUR"

Mutually expanding *Ideas* and *Selves*

ideas and vision; *pulled* to cooperation, *drawn* to genuine community, commitment, quality, productivity, and purpose. The whole (conversation, team, product, task) is often more than the sum of the contributing parts.

Indicators: Perspective on others, the task, the Self.

Fun; play; spontaneity.

Light; easy.

High productivity.

Everybody knows everybody's weaknesses and strengths.

People can laugh with others about their own weaknesses.

Solutions and communication are marked by discovery.

Creativity emerges, sometimes *explodes.*

Self-management, self-assessment, and self-correction are the norm.

Group polices itself. Leadership is a function of the whole system, not just the leader.

Self-accountability; group accountability predominantly individually self-imposed.

People often "just can't wait to get to work."

Role Clarity

Example: Quality Engineering Organization

Developed as described in Factor 12

```
                    Quality
                  Engineering
                   Supervisor
        ┌──────────────┼──────────────┐
 Mechanical/Civil   Electrical    Inspection Planning
   Supervisor       Supervisor       Supervisor
```

Mechanical/Civil Supervisor

- Interface with ANII and NRE
- Assure compliance to ASME SEC XI 1st requirements
- Review mech/civil plant procedures
- Maintain quality nonconformance control and corrective action programs
- Maintain nuclear NDE (Level III) Program
- Perform mech/civil surveillances
- Prepare SIDRS
- Maintain QAIP 15 Trend Program
- Review work request packages for QC inspection hold points
- Perform 10 CFR 50 Part 21 reviews
- Participate as quality audit team member when requested
- Participate in design reviews

Electrical Supervisor

- Provide technical accept/reject criteria for QC inspection plans
- Inspection planning and work package closure
- Review QC inspection plans
- Review initial ECN drawing package and walkdown
- Review electrical plant procedures
- Review SP and STP procedures
- Review and close electrical NCRs and CARs
- Perform NRC action item closures
- Participate as quality audit team member when requested
- Participate in design review

Inspection Planning Supervisor

- Review and approve inspection plans for maint. mod. recv. and supplier activities
- Inspection planning and work package closure
- Review work request packages
- Interface with QC
- Review QC inspection plan
- Interface with ANII for ASME code-related activities
- Review inspection procedures
- Perform quality surveillance
- Participate as quality audit team member when requested

C-1

Appendix D

Macro Performance Indicators

The following charts represent nonfinancial indicators from a plant of a major US firm. These indicators, along with financial indicators, were made available to all employees as they were continuously updated. Of course, they are keyed to the business objectives. Also, each team of employees was informed of both the organizational business objectives and the specific expectations for the team.

These indicators are called *macro* because they represent the entire plant. However, Factor 16 illustrates the development of micro measurements at the team level. As important as it is to communicate total plant indicators to the entire work force, it is even more important to have team-developed indices. These indices help make clear the expectations for each team or work group. Of course, such indices are developed with the appropriate balance of management authority and employee influence.

Between the total plant and the team measurements are the department measurements — an example follows. This charting system may appear to be complex, so you may want to develop your own charts. Simple graphs (like the macro graphs) are effective. The principle here is that people work better when they know the score.

Macro Performance Indicators

1991 Recovery

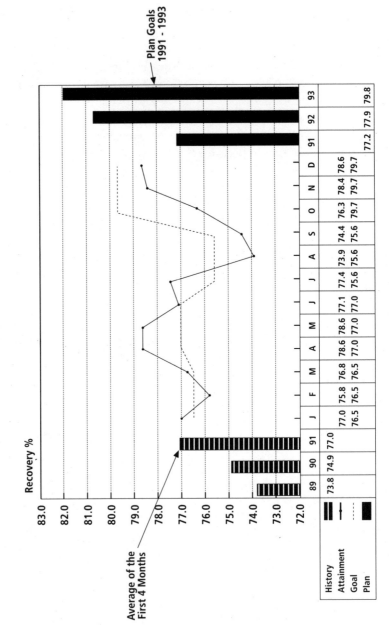

Recovery %

Plan Goals 1991 - 1993

Average of the First 4 Months

	89	90	91	J	F	M	A	M	J	J	A	S	O	N	D	91	92	93
History	73.8	74.9	77.0															
Attainment				77.0	75.8	76.8	78.6	78.6	77.1	77.4	73.9	74.4	76.3	78.4	78.6			
Goal				76.5	76.5	76.5	77.0	77.0	77.0	75.6	75.6	75.6	79.7	79.7	79.7			
Plan																77.2	77.9	79.8

Time is money. Therefore, reducing the furnace downtime (recovery) becomes a critical non-financial indicator.

D-2

Macro Performance Indicators
1991 Production

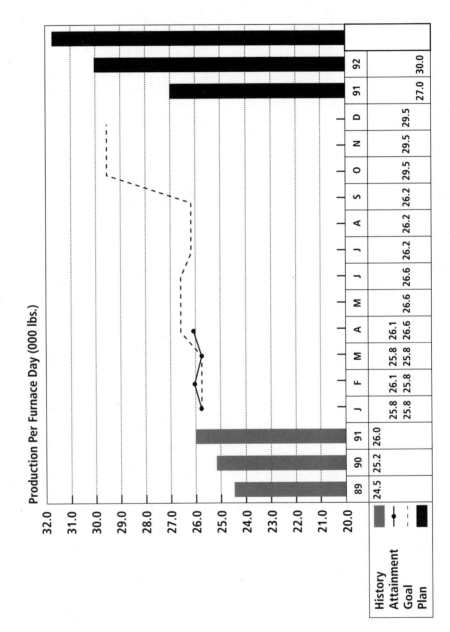

Production Per Furnace Day (000 lbs.)

	89	90	91	J	F	M	A	M	J	J	A	S	O	N	D	91	92
History	24.5	25.2	26.0														
Attainment					25.8	25.8	26.1										
Goal				25.8	26.1	25.8	26.6	26.6	26.6	26.2	26.2	26.2	29.5	29.5	29.5	27.0	30.0
Plan																	

Macro Performance Indicators

1991 Safety

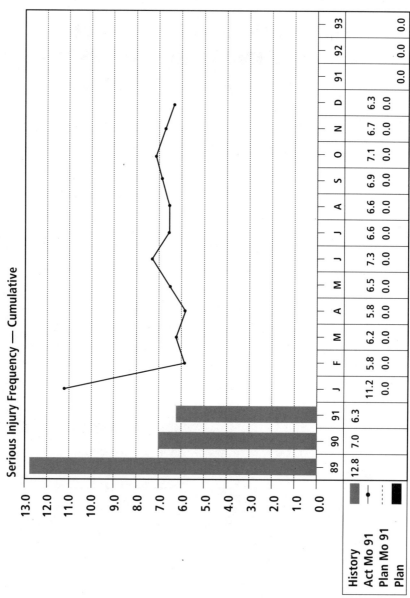

Note that the goal is zero. Also, serious injury is defined differently in different organizations. The significant feature here is that this frequency declined while other macro indicators improved. Safety, quality, and productivity are interrelated in the long run!

1991 Department Performance Indicators and Objectives*
May 1991

	Safety	Integrity	Profitability			People	Quality		← Values
No. of CBIS	Serious Injury Freq.	Bldg. 202 Emission (%)	Recovery Rate (%)	SF - 6 (Lb SF - 6 Per Lb Mag)	Control Cost 89 - 90 vs 91 % Decrease Per Lb Mag	Dept Meeting Attendance (%)	Customer Complaints Pos & Neg Remarks	Scrap (%)	
145	0	0%	93.0%	.0015	− 25.4%	100%	+ 6	1.0%	10
130	1	1%	92.0%	.0016	− 17.5%	98%	+ 5	2.0%	9
120	2	2%	91.13%	.0017	− 15%	95%	+ 4	2.5%	8
104	4	3%	91.0%	.0018	− 12.5%	92%	+ 3	3.0%	7
100	5	7.5%	90.73%	.0019	− 10.1%	90%	+ 2	3.3%	6
99	6	8.7%	90.0%	.0021	− 7.5%	88%	+ 1	3.5%	5
97	7	12%	89.0%	.0023	− 4.3%	86%	0	3.8%	4
95	8.62	24%	88.0%	.0024	0%	83%	− 1	4.5%	3†
92	10	30%	87.0%	.0033	+5%	75%	− 2	5.0%	2
89	12	40%	86%	.0035	+10%	70%	− 3	5.7%	1
85	14	50%	85%	.0038	+20%	60%	− 4	6.0%	0
10	10	5	8	4	6	10	3	1	Score
10	20	10	15	10	6	10	10	9	Weight
100	200	50	120	40	36	100	30	9	Value

Index [685]

*See Factor 16 for an explanation of this matrix.

'The "3" scores represent the average scores in the 3 months prior to Jan. 1991 and are the beginning reference point.

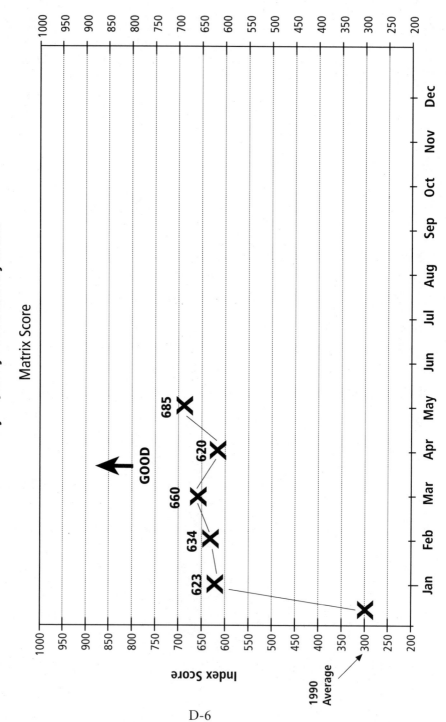

1991 Department Milestones

Safety / Quality / Productivity Index

Matrix Score

GOOD

Index Score

685
620
660
634
623

1990 Average

Jan Feb Mar Apr May Jun Jul Aug Sep Oct Nov Dec

1000 950 900 850 800 750 700 650 600 550 500 450 400 350 300 250 200

Bottom Line Costs

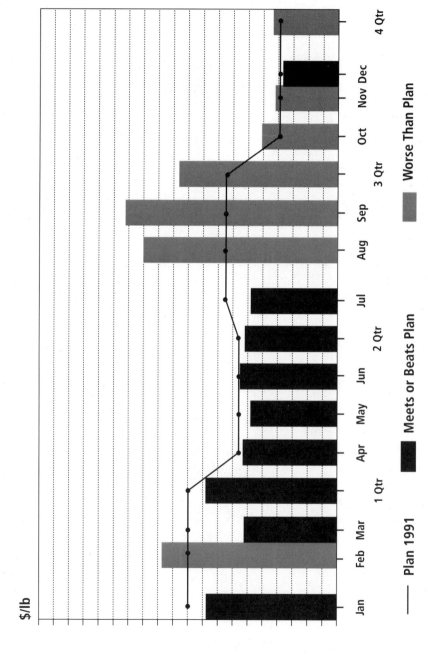

\$/lb

Jan Feb Mar Apr May Jun Jul Aug Sep Oct Nov Dec 4 Qtr
1 Qtr   2 Qtr   3 Qtr

—— Plan 1991   ▮ Meets or Beats Plan   ▮ Worse Than Plan

Higher 3rd Quarter expenditures were (under!) predicted preparatory to reaching 4th Quarter and next year's goals.

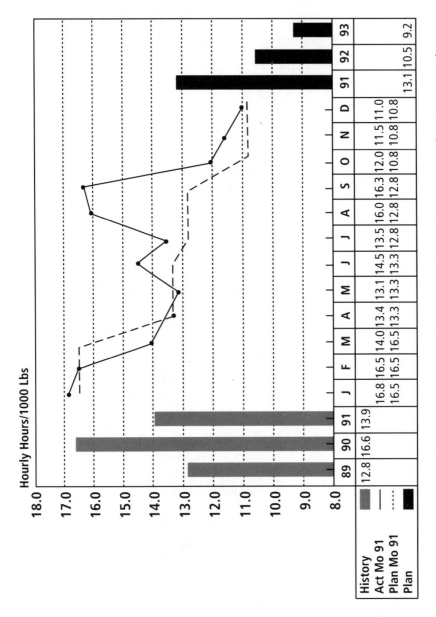

This does not reflect a reduction in hourly employees, but rather an increase in production per employee. Hourly workers will work at this capacity if managers guide them as indicated in this book.

Appendix E

High Performance Indicators
(Short Form)

1. Sponsorship

The supervisor firmly supports the group, providing resources, clarity, direction, and enthusiasm to guarantee success.

Almost Always   Almost Never

    5   4   3   2   1

2. Openness

Data flows accurately so that problems are identified. Disagreements are dealt with directly.

Almost Always   Almost Never

    5   4   3   2   1

3. Influence

Employees have input and influence on factors that impact their work life.

Almost Always   Almost Never

    5   4   3   2   1

4. Distinguish Between Decision Making and Influence

Managers are clear about the distinction between "who is deciding" versus "who is influencing" and communicate that.

Almost Always   Almost Never

5	4	3	2	1

5. Decisions Are Made

Decisions are made in an expedient amount of time.

Almost Always   Almost Never

5	4	3	2	1

6. Implementation

Decisions are effectively implemented in a timely way.

Almost Always   Almost Never

5	4	3	2	1

7. Input Needs

We get, with quality and on time, what we need from outside or inside suppliers.

Almost Always   Almost Never

5	4	3	2	1

8. Throughput

We are organized in the best possible way to produce quality output with clear and efficient processes.

Almost Always				Almost Never
5	4	3	2	1

9. Output

We give to others, with quality and on time, what they need and provide excellent service.

Almost Always				Almost Never
5	4	3	2	1

10. Meetings

Our meetings are effective.

Almost Always				Almost Never
5	4	3	2	1

11. Creativity

New ideas for improving work processes, communication, product development, etc., are encouraged.

Almost Always				Almost Never
5	4	3	2	1

12. Job Clarity

I know exactly what I am to do.

Almost Always   Almost Never

5	4	3	2	1

13. Person-Task Fit

The right people are doing the right tasks.

Almost Always   Almost Never

5	4	3	2	1

14. Authority

People have the authority to do what they are expected to do.

Almost Always   Almost Never

5	4	3	2	1

15. Resource Availability

We are able to get the resources we need to do our job well.

Almost Always   Almost Never

5	4	3	2	1

16. Team Measurements

We are able regularly to measure key factors related to our input, throughput, and output so that we can monitor and quickly problem-solve low-scoring items.

Almost Always				Almost Never
5	4	3	2	1

17. Big-Picture Perspective

We know the larger picture and on everyday tasks we know why we are doing what we are doing.

Almost Always				Almost Never
5	4	3	2	1

18. Training

Members of our work team are well trained.

Almost Always				Almost Never
5	4	3	2	1

19. Priorities

Priorities are consistently clear.

Almost Always				Almost Never
5	4	3	2	1

20. By-whens

Whenever a decision is made, someone clarifies who will do what and by when.

Almost Always   Almost Never

5	4	3	2	1

21. Follow-Through

Commitments are effectively tracked.

Almost Always   Almost Never

5	4	3	2	1

22. Single-Point Accountability

There is one person accountable for each task.

Almost Always   Almost Never

5	4	3	2	1

23. Reinforcement

People are appreciated for work well done.

Almost Always   Almost Never

5	4	3	2	1

24. Reprimands

Reprimands are clear and very specific about the unappreciated work or action but not accusatory, judgmental, or vindictive.

Almost Always   Almost Never

5	4	3	2	1

25. Work Relationships

Work relationships are maintained by being direct.

Almost Always   Almost Never

5	4	3	2	1

Appendix F

An Example of One Industry's Adaptation of the 25 Factors to Fit Its Values and Needs

The following illustrates part of an adaptation by one industry of the 25 Factors in this book. The Factors were expanded (producing 42 questions) and were grouped by the six value areas of the company. What follows illustrates how questions were added in the value area *Quality and Excellence*. Note that scales 6-9 are from the 25 Factors. Items 1-5 are added.

Quality and Excellence

1. All employees know who their customers are.

   Almost Always   Almost Never
   _____
   5   4   3   2   1

2. Customer satisfaction is given high priority.

   Almost Always   Almost Never
   _____
   5   4   3   2   1

3. All employees are familiar with the company Quality Improvement Process.

   Almost Always   Almost Never
   _____
   5   4   3   2   1

4. All employees have had some quality training in the last 12 months.

Almost Always   Almost Never
_____

        5   4   3   2   1

5. You are a member of a quality team.

Almost Always   Almost Never
_____

        5   4   3   2   1

6. Input needs

We get, with quality and on time, what we need from outside or inside suppliers.

Almost Always   Almost Never
_____

        5   4   3   2   1

7. Throughput

We are organized in the best possible way to produce quality output with clear and efficient processes.

Almost Always   Almost Never
_____

        5   4   3   2   1

8. Output

We give to others, with quality and on time, what they need and provide excellent service.

Almost Always   Almost Never

    5   4   3   2   1

9. Resource Availability

We are able to get the sources we need to do our job well.

Almost Always   Almost Never

    5   4   3   2   1

Appendix G

Specificity Quiz

Too often organization effectiveness suffers as a result of language that, though intended as factual, is subject to various interpretations. Engineers in their reports, supervisors in giving feedback, quality inspectors, employees attempting to be clear about concerns — all confuse phrases that *make a judgment* from those that *report a fact.* And this coloring of fact often gives rise to conflict: "You're being careless" versus "Three jars were broken this past hour." "The second shift isn't working hard" versus "Production is down 40 cases today compared to yesterday."

A differentiated person makes this distinction and strives to communicate with specificity. The judgment/interpretation not only inflames, but, worse, it draws attention and energy from the problem (i.e., three jars were broken) and focuses on the accusation.

In the following quiz, see how well you can distinguish between being factual or interpretive. In other words, distinguish between nonjudgmental and judgmental statements. Review the 18 statements that follow and put an "X" beside each one that you consider to be specific, that is, an observable fact rather than an interpretation.

Specificity Quiz

1. (_____) Joe was not being professional.

2. (_____) Harry was sincere.

3. (_____) Harry misinterpreted Joe.

4. (_____) Joe was discouraged.

5. (_____) Harry's voice got louder when he said, "Cut it out, Joe."

6. (_____) Joe was trying to make Harry angry.

7. (_____) Harry talked more than Joe did.

8. (_____) Joe was aggressive.

9. (_____) Joe said nothing when Harry said, "Cut it out."

10. (_____) Harry knew that Joe was feeling discouraged.

11. (_____) Joe talked about the weather and the baseball game.

12. (_____) Jane deliberately changed the subject.

13. (_____) Bill forgot the meeting.

14. (_____) Harry did not show respect to his boss.

15. (_____) That is the third time you have started to talk while I was talking.

16. (_____) The furnace repair was inadequate.

17. (_____) The thermostat was set at 180°.

18. (_____) I expect to receive this report by 3 PM tomorrow.

Specificity Quiz — Responses and Rationale[34]

1. Joe was not being professional. (Inference)

    The word "professional" carries a *value connotation*. It is an interpretation not a fact. While there may be general agreement on abstract qualities of what it means to be a professional (e.g., courteous, punctual, etc.), there are wide differences about how those abstracts translate into minute-by-minute, day-by-day behavior in specific incidents. Does a professional raise his voice when he is angry or does he speak softly? How does a professional dress? If someone wanted Joe to change (from not being professional), he/she must be specific.

2. Harry was sincere. (Inference)

    We can never know for sure whether others are sincere or insincere. We can know that they speak in a solemn tone; we can see that their faces do not wear a smile; we can observe that they repeated themselves twice with emphasis. All these could be facts, but to infer from this that they are being sincere or insincere is an opinion/ judgment/inference.

3. Harry misinterpreted Joe. (Inference)

    We could state what Harry said after hearing Joe, but we would not know if that were a misinterpretation without further data.

4. Joe was discouraged. (Inference)

    This is an inference about someone else's emotional state. You can observe that Joe put his head down or that Joe spoke in a low voice, but you cannot know if he was discouraged. You can presume it, but you cannot know it without checking with Joe.

---

[34] Revised by Robert Crosby from original work done by John Wallen.

5. Harry's voice got louder when he said, "Cut it out, Joe." — (Specific)

   You can hear a voice get louder and you can hear a person say, "Cut it out, Joe." Notice there is not inference about this. It does not say that Harry misinterpreted Joe or that he was sincere or that Joe had just interrupted Harry. None of the evaluative words are in this sentence, so this is descriptive.

6. Joe was trying to make Harry angry. (Inference)

   Again, we do not know Joe's intention, so this is interpretative, judgmental, and nondescriptive.

7. Harry talked more than Joe. (Specific)

   A fact. That is, somebody talked more than the other. Who was that person? There is *no* value judgment. If either Harry or Joe are unhappy with their own participation, they may view this fact as a judgment. Nevertheless, it is not a judgment.

8. Joe was aggressive. (Inference)

   What appears to be aggressive behavior to one person is called assertive by another. Sometimes a behavior done by a woman is called aggressive (or other choice words) whereas that same behavior by a man is called assertive or manly. So the same behavior may be admired or not, depending on how it fits our prejudice (prejudgment) of how a certain person should behave.

9. Joe said nothing when Harry said, "Cut it out." (Specific)

   A verifiable fact; observable silence.

10. Harry knew that Joe was feeling discouraged. (Inference)

11. Joe talked about the weather and the baseball game. (Specific)

12. Jane deliberately changed the subject. (Judgment)

    Jane may have changed the subject, but whether she did so deliberately involves a judgment. She may have done it inadvertently or simply because she thought that the discussion of the previous topic was completed.

13. Bill forgot the meeting. (Inference)

    This is a fact only if Bill tells us so (and is telling the truth). He may simply have chosen not to come. Therefore, this is an inference.

14. Harry did not show respect to his boss. (Inference)

    Respect means many different things. For example, to many bosses respect means being willing to express disagreements directly to the boss, while for others it means the opposite. One maintenance group, when pushed for specificity, said they would feel "respected" if they were consulted prior to the purchase of certain, specified equipment with which they had extensive experience and competence.

15. That is the third time you have started to talk while I was talking. (Specific)

    This can be verified.

16. The furnace repair was inadequate. (Interpretive)

    Inadequate by what criteria?

17. The thermostat was set at 180.° (Specific)

18. I expect to receive this report by 3 PM tomorrow. (Specific)

Appendix H

Brainstorming Rules

1. Take turns.

2. One idea per turn. Say "pass" if you have no idea and continue the activity until all have said "pass."

3. Say anything that comes to mind — in *short* phrases or a few words.

4. Recorder writes down exactly what is said — no editing. Clarity will come after brainstorming is complete.

5. Do not discuss ideas at the time they are offered.

6. No evaluations or judgments, positive or negative.

7. Repetition is okay.

8. Go for quantity, not quality or accuracy. Those are later tasks.

9. Have fun!

Note: Brainstorming is intended to tap into the creative right brain and spontaneity is a part of that. Do not get into linear thinking, i.e., reading from a list. However, if people seem *stuck,* have them separately take a few, quiet minutes to themselves to make a list of a *few* items to add to the brainstormed list. Then, proceed as above.

Appendix I

Action Recommendations/Commitments

Problem Statement	Recommended Action	To Be Done By Whom	Comments	Date By-When Complete or Reviewed

Appendix J

Characteristics of an Effective Facilitator

- Empowered by sponsor

- Assertive: Can take charge

- Neutral on substantive issues

- High skill in conflict resolution

- High skill in the problem-solving process

- High skill in being clear

- High skill in guiding the meeting

- Differentiated

Appendix K

Orientation Session

1. Greet participants as they arrive. Have an informal, semi-circle chair arrangement. Make introductions. Do *not* invite questions at this time. Share the big-picture of your organization, including your business objectives (perhaps for the next quarter) and values (e.g., customer satisfaction, employee involvement, etc.) that are important to achieve. (See Factor 17.) Make clear that this survey feedback activity is expected to be a means to those ends. You may want to describe directions such as are illustrated by Display One, *Examples of Cultural Shifts,* at the end of this Appendix.

2. Do not talk more than 10 minutes without having participants form pairs to discuss their responses and reactions to your statements. Then ask for brief comments or questions.

   Invite people to pair with someone with whom they rarely talk. Give them 3-5 minutes. Do this periodically during the orientation session in order to increase clarity and demonstrate a balance between your input and their participation.

3. You might ask the question, "What is this session all about? For one thing, it is about influence. It is about everyone being more influential. What do employees need to influence?"

   Employees need to influence:

   • Clarity about my job.

   • Clarity about:

       . . . any special projects I am assigned.
       . . . who decides what.
       . . . how I am doing.

- Ability to get:

    ... commitments from others.
    ... the information I need to do my job.
    ... the materials or resources needed to excel.
    ... equipment fixed in a timely manner.

- Ability to impact productivity and quality issues.

- Ability to influence decisions that affect me, such as:

    ... the amount of space I have.
    ... space decor, ventilation, temperature, and noise.
    ... work redesign.
    ... lighting, space arrangement, etc.
    ... procedures and processes.
    ... equitable compensation.
    ... purchases of equipment I use.
    ... measurements of my work.
    ... schedules.
    ... openness about what is and is not working.

You might ask, "Is there anything missing from this list? If motivation is low in your company, the odds are very high that people are not influential in the above areas.

4. Continue with intermittant pairings. After the above (#3) input, ask them to talk about influence. Specifically, "What do you need to be able to influence more to get your job done?"

5. After five minutes, ask if one pair will share their discussion with the entire group. You are *not* asking for a detailed report of the paired discussion but for the highlights. Listen. Paraphrase. Create a dialogue. Do not persuade. Do not promise success. This is not a problem-solving session but an attempt to illustrate the kinds of issues that may be worked on in the coming survey feedback process.

6. Ask those who have participated in a survey process that seemed similar to this to raise their hands. Ask, "Of those who have your hands up, how many saw the data that was fed back to your company?" Continue asking those who have their hands up: "How many had data fed back to your immediate work group?" "How many had an opportunity to work with that data and prioritize concerns?" "How many got to develop action recommendations from those concerns?" "How many got to give these to your supervisor and had timely decisions made?" "How many had follow-through sessions?" By now probably all hands are down. Make the point that all of the steps mentioned in the questions just asked are a part of this activity.

7. Create a new pairing.

8. Summarize the survey feedback steps. Illustrate visually on a flip chart or chalkboard. Include dates. For example:

   a. Orientation (today's meeting) — Administration of the survey.

   b. Data Feedback and Problem Solving (one or two days — time and date).

   c. Discuss recommendations with boss (2 hours — time and date; this may be done on the same day as b).

   d. Boss responds and action plans are outlined (time and date; also may be done on same day as b and c).

   e. Follow-through activities (times and dates).

9. Have new pairs discuss the steps outlined in item 7 above.

10. Invite questions for clarity.

11. Administer the survey. Explain the scale and how the scores are compiled. Talk again about who sees the compiled data and when they will see it.

Display One

Examples of Cultural Shifts

From		Toward
(The way it once was or may still be)		(The way we want it to be)
• Finding fault and blame	→	"Make it work" — take responsibility
• Language of "I'll try"	→	"I'll do it"
• Low trust and morale	→	High trust and morale
• Low concern for safety	→	Excellent safety record
• People who use and repair have no input on equipment purchase	→	These people have input prior to decision being made
• No by-whens (clear completion dates)	→	By-whens
• No clear accountability	→	Single-point accountability is in place
• It is unclear who decides what	→	Authority about decision making is clear
• Shoot the messenger	→	Honor the messenger even if the message is difficult to hear
• Not able to get materials when needed	→	Able to get materials when needed

A scale of 1 (low) to 10 (high) has been used to score cultural items such as those listed above. A gain of 3 to 4 points can be expected when following a strategy that includes a well-done survey feedback component. At the beginning, expect the average score to be 2 to 4. (Example: In the last category, "not able to get materials . . . ," a score of 1 represents the worst possible condition and a 10, the best possible.)

Appendix L

Data Feedback and Problem-Solving Session

1. Greet people and explain the purpose of the session and the function of the data, that is, both to surface areas of strength and to identify issues to problem-solve, not to find blame. State (as manager) your expectations of the results of the session. Then, ask for and listen to concerns people have about the process or data.

2. If a facilitator is being used to conduct the problem solving, introduce her/him and explain the facilitator's role, or ask her/him to elaborate on the role. The facilitator is to guide the process, not interpret the data. The group makes its own interpretations. If you are facilitating the meeting, offer the data in the same way, reserving your interpretation until the group has formed its own.

3. Share the data or have the facilitator guide the group through the data. (The more complex the survey and the lower the scores, the greater the need for a facilitator). The data is to be shared *totally* at first. There are to be no interpretations by anyone, either positive or negative, at this point. Go through the questions one by one, asking people to mark the factors (both strengths and problems) that are important to them. Reserve discussion until all the data is shared, except for *brief* comments for clarity as you go.

4. Ask people to comment on the strengths or areas of high scores in order to set the tone for the day.

5. Guide (or have the facilitator guide) the team in prioritizing the hot issues on which to work.

   a. Begin by posting a list of the Factors that have been identified by the group as possible problems.

   b. Divide the number of Factors on this list by four to determine the number of votes for each person.

c. Record the number of votes received for each Factor.

d. Take the top five Factors and ask everyone to pick their top two choices of these five. Post the totals. The Factors with the most votes will be the prioritized items on which the team will work. Other Factors may be on the agenda for later follow-through sessions.

6. Before you work on a priority, determine if that Factor is:

a. chronic and/or complex and not likely to be improved by a simple solution (for example, Factors 2, 8, and 18).

b. perhaps not simple but likely to be improved by following the suggestions in Chapter 3 (for example, Factors 13, 14, 16, 19, and 20). If so, skip the instructions for the chronic/complex issues.

c. simple (for example, the boss agrees to be clear about the decision-making style being used, and the employees agree to ask for clarification if the style being used is not apparent). (See Factor 4 for clarity about the concept of decision-making styles.) If so, skip the instructions for the chronic/complex issues.

Furthermore, if the Factor is complex and/or chronic and you are part of a larger organization, then it most likely is a system issue and must, for effective resolution, be addressed in and by the system. In this case the boss may agree to initiate action on this issue in the larger system. Of course, work on a chronic and/or complex issue requires more thorough analysis. Follow the instructions for chronic/complex issues.

7. Instructions for chronic and/or complex issues.

a. Write the priority Factor at the top of the flip chart. Explain that you are going to look for obstacles that sustain the problem (no solutions yet). But first, ask for specific examples of the Factor. Ask for one word or short phrases only, and then begin brainstorming obstacles. Follow the *Brainstorming Rules* (see Appendix H) to get maximum input.

 b. Review the brainstormed list of obstacles for clarity. As you go through the list of items, invite the person who offered the item to clarify and give specific examples as needed.

 c. Then prioritize the items. Do not rank order them but reduce the list to those items that are seen as most important and solvable.

 d. Next, brainstorm possible solutions to all of the important and solvable items. (Do *not* brainstorm each item separately. It takes too much time and does not add to the *quality* of the solutions.)

 e. Have the group assist in clarifying and categorizing these solutions. During this step ask people for specific examples of where, when, and how the solution will be applied.

 f. Choose your desired solutions and reword them to create recommendations that are behaviorally specific, not general, and are directed to a particular person (sometimes the manager, sometimes others). This allows the identified person to respond directly and give a commitment and date (by-when) for follow-through. If it involves someone outside of the group, the manager's role is to take the recommendation to the appropriate person.

8. Record all recommendations, agreements, actions, and by-whens to facilitate follow-up. A simple form or log will assist with this. (See the sample form in Appendix I.) Many recommendations may include actions by members of the group itself to change a particular process or way of working. Commitments should be recorded, indicating both by-when and by-whom the action will be taken.

9. Recommendations are then presented to the manager. If the manager has not been present during the problem solving and writing of the recommendations, he/she joins the group and each person takes a turn presenting a recommendation to the manager.

The manager asks questions first for clarity, then responds to the recommendations he/she can accept *now* with a by-when commitment. He/she then takes other recommendations under advisement and gives a date when he/she can get back to the group with an answer/response or a progress report. The manager may need more data in order to make a decision and may ask a team/group member to assist in gathering that data. Also, agreements from the group to the manager are recorded. For example, if people request that the manager clarify his/her decision style when making certain work requests, the reciprocal agreement will be that the employees will ask for clarity when that style is not clear. That agreement should be recorded.

Appendix M

Follow-Up Meetings

The follow-up meetings are a critical part of the success of survey feed-back. The meetings need to be experienced as being as important as the problem-solving step. New issues may emerge at each follow-up session. Following are steps for conducting these sessions:

A. The manager and team members are all present.

B. The manager or facilitator asks each person to score how well each item has been completed or what progress has been made. Have a copy of agreements or recommendations for each person. Have people individually rate each agreement using a scale of 1 (low) to 10 (high). Go quickly through this activity, without discussion. When all items have been scored, collect the sheets and post the scores on the flip chart.

C. Discuss each recommendation and its score separately, asking for specifics on what is working and what is not; e.g., if someone scored an item 2 and another gave it a score of 10, why? What are the different experiences? What is working for some and not for others? New problems may emerge for consideration. Also, and equally important, there will be a common understanding and appreciation of what *is* working and changing.

D. Make any assignments or schedule necessary problem-solving meetings for any new problems that have surfaced and add them to the Recommendation/Action form. This is a dynamic, evolving document when used at all follow-up sessions.

E. Schedule (or reinforce) the date for the next follow-up meeting and religiously keep this date. Many survey feedback processes break down at this point. Some organizations/teams fold this process/list into regular team meetings. However, two or three (minimum) meetings devoted solely to survey feedback follow-up are necessary to establish a norm.

Appendix N

An Exercise in Distinguishing Between Openness and Personal Confession

To operate at their peak both individuals and organizations need to be open. Only with openness does data flow through organizations with the speed and clarity needed to cope with change. But the concept of openness can sound threatening when people confuse *being open* with *personal confession.*[35]

There is a vital difference between these two concepts. The following exercise will help you to clarify the difference. Personal confession is the sharing of private, personal information about one's self. It is often about past events. Openness, on the other hand, is about clearly describing what is happening *now.*

With *openness* feedback is very specific, clear, descriptive, and timely ("I liked the fact that you condensed your summary to one page"). In *personal confession* people talk about their personal life. Conversation in a personal confession is from one's private, internal experience.

With *openness* the data that flows deals with the immediate situation. "You're asking me for this report by Wednesday noon, but I do not think I can finish it by then." That is the openness organizations need. With *personal confession* norms predominating, such feedback is often withheld for fear of hurting feelings, being hurt, or being too *personal.* Such confusion between openness (which organizations need) and personal confession (which is appropriate with a counselor or differentiated friend) encourages closed behavior that negatively affects organizations.

---

[35] John Wallen did the initial work in this area. Robert Crosby teamed with Wallen in the late 60s and early 70s in a series of Laboratory Training Sessions. This adaptation uses examples from industry.

Exercise

With the above as background, take a few minutes with this exercise to distinguish between *personal confession* and *openness*. Here are 10 items followed by an explanation. Put a check mark if you think the statement is an example of openness; leave it blank if you think it illustrates personal confession.

1. _____ "Damn it Joe, I expected your report an hour ago!"

Congratulations if you put a check mark here. To be open in the purest sense, a statement reflects the speaker's feelings and is specific about the activity. While "Damn it Joe" does not contain a feeling word (e.g., I'm angry), the hearer will easily get the message if the *tone* fits.

In real life tone and words often do not match. Perhaps the speaker has trouble being clear about feelings and therefore says, "Damn it Joe," in a light, jovial way. Such a double message is often sent. When *tone* and *message* do not match, people usually believe the *tone.*

If the tone were jovial, the facial expressions would be too — some 85% of communication is facial/tonal. The outcome of a series of communications where such a facial/tonal message conflicts with the words is that the sender eventually explodes with, "I've told you this over and over!" The receiver responds, "I thought you were kidding!"

(Of course, tone is not present in this exercise, so let us assume that tone and words match when doing this exercise.)

2. _____ "I've always had trouble being on time."

No check here. This is a personal confession of one's history. As the statement stands, you cannot tell whether the speaker is defending or is upset with him/herself, or what. You also are not sure whether the reference is to a specific lateness or whether it is simply a general statement.

3. _____ "Frankly, I'm having a rough time with my marriage."

No check here. This is clearly a personal confession. We are not claiming that personal confessions are not sometimes appropriate to share. We are claiming that the mainstream sharing of information at work should be openness about work activities and their effect on you and others.

Occasionally private, personal sharing is important, but one should clearly know the difference and know that the result of sharing personal information is that the relationship with the *hearer* shifts, at least temporarily, to that of counselee/counselor. Thus, *if you choose to be personal, choose your counselors wisely.*

4. _____ "Thanks for getting those estimates to me on time and well documented."

Yes, a check here! The feelings are clearly inferred by the "thanks," and the work activity is spelled out. Furthermore, this example illustrates why openness is important in organizations. Openness is about dataflow. Data must flow accurately, on time, in the form needed, and with clear expectations.

5. _____ "I'm beginning to tune out with all the details in your report."

A check belongs here. Feelings are clear and specific about the activity.

6. _____ "You're irresponsible."

No check here. This is a parental statement. No feelings are shared though one certainly can infer negative ones. Mainly missing is specificity. This is an excellent example of a projective statement that will evoke defensiveness and probably a counter-attack. If the hearer is subordinate, the counter-attack will likely be out of the hearing of the superior.

Actually, this is neither open nor a personal confession. It is an accusation. It is an unintended *confession* by the one who charges, "You're irresponsible." It says that responsibility is a big word in the speaker's life history. Another observer might say, "You're selfish." Still another, "You're forthright" and another, "You're courageous." And the irony is that all these responses might be evoked by the same behavior.

In the movie, *Twelve Angry Men,* all of the jurors project unresolved issues in their own lives onto the young man on trial. This *eye of the beholder* phenomena is at work whether the speaker calls the other person "irresponsible," "selfish," "forthright," or "courageous." These accusations tell us not about the person spoken to but about the person speaking. That is why we call it a projective statement.

7. _____   "I work best when you tell me expected results first, cost estimates second, and the project plans third."

Yes, a check. Another excellent example of the direct relationship between openness and productivity/quality.

8. _____   "I'm seeing a counselor regularly."

No check. This is clearly a personal confession.

9. _____   "I like the way we solved the problem of that production issue."

Yes, a check. There is specificity about both feelings and the activity.

10. _____   "It's important to me to have the delivery made at the expected time or to be given a day's notice of a possible delay."

Yes, a check. Once again, specificity about feelings ("important to me" infers the feeling) and the activity.

That completes the exercise, but there is more about the discrepancy between tonal/facial expressions and words. First, do this: Say, "Thanks a lot," in a sarcastic tone. That will illustrate how much more powerful tone is than words. Of course, nobody would feel thanked with such a tone.

The point *is not* to try to match your tone to the words but to believe the tone and realize that the words need to be re-examined. Unrehearsed tone does not lie. So, when the words and tone do not match, review the words if you want to be true to yourself. Review them to *discover* what you truly believe about the issue at hand.

On Being Authentic

One of the greatest gifts one can give oneself is to take a deep breath and reflect on feedback; it is the pause that refreshes and cleanses the stress of duplicity from life. So, change words to match tone, not vice versa. Reassess the truth about yourself revealed through your tone.

Being an authentic person is to be one whose tone and words match not by faking *tone* but by being clear about the words you want to say. You may believe that such authenticity is not practical or possible in your situation. So be it! The words on this page and the openness prescribed in this book are for those who are choosing to "be the truth" in *openness*. Then your tone and words will match without theatrics. As Soren Kierkegard, the Danish philosopher, put it, "The truth consists, not in knowing the truth, but in being the truth."

The Challenge of Learning Openness

Openness is essential if data is to flow freely through organizations. Learning openness requires training in differentiation. Differentiation is a prerequisite skill not only to *resolve* but to *utilize* conflict well.[36]

To be open is to be specific, concrete, and nonjudgmental rather than general and judgmental. A primary commitment of a person in an open organization is to "tell it like it is" — not in the old school sense of being judgmental and accusative but in the new sense of being specific and nonjudgmental and toward the end of achieving the organizational mission. A true leader is the one who will describe life's situations without blaming others. The goal is to *make it work* rather than *find fault or blame.*

Differentiated training goes beyond that which all but the boldest organizations care to take on today. But the willingness to take on such training will define those organizations that are the most productive while also being the most humane. We need to have folks whose skills go beyond just those needed to get minimal work done. We need to equip a manager to become a mentor, a teacher, a wise person, who by word, tone, and deed displays the very heart and soul of an open, productive organization. And that manager will balance management authority and employee influence.

---

[36] Our thanks to Ronald Lippitt for helping shift the concept "managing conflict" to "utilizing conflict." He wisely saw that differences of opinion are potential riches to be mined or utilized — not simply "managed" to reduce the conflict.

Appendix O

The Interpersonal Gap[37]

by John L. Wallen

You cannot have your own way all the time. Your best intentions will sometimes end in disaster, while at other times you will receive credit for desirable outcomes you did not intend. In short, what you accomplish is not always what you hoped for.

Why does this happen? The most basic and recurring problems in social life stem from the disparity between what you intend and the actual effect of your actions on others. The key terms we use in attempting to make sense of interpersonal relations are "intentions," "actions," and "effects." "Interpersonal Gap" refers to the degree of congruence between one person's intentions and the effect produced in the other. If the effect is what was intended, the gap has been bridged. If the effect is the opposite of what was intended, the gap has become greater. Let us look more closely at these three terms.

Intentions

Intentions mean the conscious wishes, wants, hopes, desires, and fears that give rise to action. It does not refer to the underlying motives of which one is unaware. It is a fact that people can tell you after an action has produced some result, "That wasn't what I meant to do." Or, "Yes, that's exactly what I hoped would happen." We look at the social outcome and decide whether it is what we intended. Apparently we can compare what we wished prior to acting with the outcome after we have acted and determine whether they match.

---

[37] As published in *Inside Out* (formerly the *Navigator*), John Scherer & Assoc., Spokane, WA, Winter 1991. Written in the 1960s, this is a major foundational article in communications theory.

Here are some examples of interpersonal intentions:

- "I want him to like me."
- "I want her to do what I say."
- "I want him to realize that I know a great deal about this subject."
- "I don't want her to know that I am disappointed in her."
- "I wish she would tell me what to do."
- "I wish I could get him off the phone."

Intentions may also be mixed. For example:

- "I want him to know I like him, but I don't want to be embarrassed."
- "I want her to tell me I'm doing a good job, but I don't want to ask for it."
- "I would like him to know how angry I get when he does that, but I don't want to lose his friendship."
- "How can I get my boss to see that her idea won't work, without making her angry with me?"

Intentions are private and are known directly only to the one who has them. I know my own intentions, but I must infer yours. You know your own intentions, but you must infer mine.

Effect/Interpretation

"Effect" refers to a person's inner response to the actions of another. It is his/her *interpretation*. We may describe the effect by openly stating what feelings are aroused by the action. However, we are often unaware of our feelings as feelings. This influences how we see the other person. We may label him/her or the action in a way that expresses those unidentified feelings.

A's Actions → Effect in **B** → How **B** may talk about the effect of **A**'s actions

Example:

A lectures **B**. **B** feels hurt, put down, angry. "When **A** acts like that, I resent him." Or, "**A** is smug and arrogant."

Below are three additional examples of two ways of responding to the same effect: by *describing* one's own feelings and by *expressing* one's own feelings by labeling the other person.

1. **Describing feelings:**

    "I got irritated with him when he did that."

    Expressing feelings by labeling the other:

    "He's self-centered. He wanted to hurt me."

2. **Describing feelings:**

    "After what she just did, I feel closer and more trusting of her."

    Expressing feelings by labeling the other:

    "She's certainly a warm, understanding person."

3. **Describing feelings:**

    "When he acts like that I feel embarrassed and ill-at-ease."

    Expressing feelings by labeling the other:

    "He's loud and obnoxious."

Actions

In contrast to interpersonal intentions and effects, which are private, actions are most often public and observable. They may be verbal ("Hi, how are things?") or nonverbal (looking away when passing another); brief (handing someone a memo) or extended (taking a person out to dinner or calling a meeting).

All interactions are communicative. They include attempts by the sender to convey a message, whether or not it is received, as well as actions that the receiver responds to as messages, whether or not the sender intended them that way. The message is in the eye — and ear — of the beholder.

Here is a schematic summary of the interpersonal gap:

> **A**'s private intentions are transformed into → **A**'s observable actions are transformed into → Private effects in **B.**

The interpersonal gap contains two transformations: first the encoding and then the decoding operations. **A**'s actions are an encoded expression of his or her inner state. **B**'s inner response is a result of the way he or she decodes **A**'s actions. If **B** decodes **A**'s behavior in the same way that **A** has coded it, **A** will have produced the effect he/she intended.

To be specific, let us imagine that I feel friendly and trusting toward you. I pat you on the shoulder. The pat is an action code for my friendly feelings. You decode this, however, as an act of condescension. The effect is that you feel put down, inferior, and annoyed with me. My system of encoding does not match your system of decoding and consequently, the interpersonal gap is present.

We can now draw a more complete picture of the interpersonal gap as shown in the following diagram.

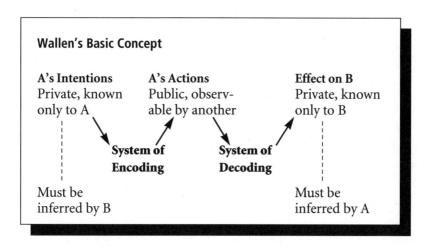

Wallen's Basic Concept

A's Intentions	A's Actions	Effect on B
Private, known only to A	Public, observable by another	Private, known only to B

System of **Encoding**

System of **Decoding**

Must be inferred by B

Must be inferred by A

You may be unaware of the ways you encode your intentions and decode other's actions. In fact, you may have been unaware that you even do this. One of the important objectives of this study of interpersonal communication is to help you become aware of the silent assumptions that influence how you encode and decode your actions and the actions of others.

If you are aware of your decoding operation, you can accurately describe the impact other people have on you when they do certain things. If you are unaware of your method of decoding the behavior of others, you cannot accurately describe the kinds of distortions or misreadings of others you typically make. Some people, for example, respond to gestures of appreciation as if they were attempts to limit their autonomy. Some respond to offers of help as if they were being put down. Some misread enthusiasm or fear as anger.

The Ambiguity of Actions

Because different people use different codes, actions have no unique and constant meaning in themselves. A similar intention may give rise to a range of different actions, such as the following:

Intention	Actions
To show affection.	Take her out to dinner.
	Buy him a gift.
	Show interest in what she says.
	Do not interrupt him when he is busy or preoccupied.

By the same token different intentions may be expressed by the same action.

Intentions	Action
To put them in your debt.	Take them out to dinner.
To sweeten a business deal.	
To repay a social obligation.	
To get closer to her.	
To impress him.	

Now, follow that single action to its conclusion. In this confusing system of communication, the same act may lead to wildly different results.

Action	Effects
A takes B out to dinner.	B feels uneasy; thinks, "I wonder what A really wants from me?"
	B enjoys it; thinks, "A really likes me."
	B feels scornful. "A is trying to impress me."
	B feels uncomfortable and ashamed. "I never did anything like this for A."

Just as a single action may produce several effects, several different actions may lead to the same effect. For example:

Actions	Effect
A tells **B** she showed **B**'s report to top administration.	**B** feels proud and happy. "**A** recognizes my competence and ability."
A tells **B** he has been doing an excellent job.	
A asks **B** for advice.	
A gives **B** a raise.	

It should be obvious that when you and I interact, each of us views our own and the other's actions in a different frame of reference. We see our own actions in the light of our own intentions, but we see the other's actions not in light of the other person's intentions but in the effect on us.

This is the principle of partial information — *each party to an interaction has different and partial information that creates a gap in understanding.* Bridging this interpersonal gap requires that each person fathom how the other sees the interaction.

Appendix P

Managing Meetings of Matrixed Task Forces/Committees for Results

Meetings of task forces, project teams, and committees are a hologram of an organization. Take the temperature there and you can predict the behavior of the prevailing culture. Let me illustrate by listing some major themes of a successful results-oriented group.

1. **Clarity about Sponsorship**

   Who sponsors this work? The sponsor must be clearly identified and active in the sponsoring function. That includes having reasonable clarity about goals and getting clear with other supporting sponsors.[38] In addition, the sponsor is active in identifying the scope of the work, the single-point accountability (especially critical in matrixed groups), and the membership of the group. The sponsor is also involved in the preplanning of key elements, such as the facilitator selection, effective use of technical resources, and consequence management.

2. **Facilitation Selection**

   The knee-jerk choice of a facilitator is often to have either the highest ranking boss or a technical expert take charge. Yet a major criteria for choosing a facilitator is one's ability to be neutral about outcomes. It is possible for a gifted and trained person to act neutral even if he or she does not feel neutral. I have seen a highly trained and skilled facilitator literally switch hats as he moved back and forth from the facilitation role to a proactive, subject-expert role.

   However, if an organization values a free exchange of differing ideas, then performing two roles is likely to result in a double loss.

---

[38] By definition, a matrixed group has members reporting to different sponsors. Single-point accountability (see the Action Idea for Factor 22) and alignment at the sponsor level is crucial to success.

Effective facilitation will be lost, and the technical resources of the person juggling both roles will probably be diluted.

An organization needs a trained cadre of internal employees who can function effectively as facilitators of specialized meetings. This cadre might include both managers and line employees. I have seen line employees, after training, effectively lead groups that included line managers.

3. **Effective Use of Technical Resources**

    Technical organizations are notoriously bad in this area. The assumption that technical discussion is only rational and not emotional is the achilles heel of such groups. The emotionality of analytically-oriented groups is expressed by challenging others before checking to see if one understands, by long theoretical explanations (defenses) when disagreement appears, or, worse, by avoiding the apparent difference and by lapsing into deferent behavior.

    Technical experts, when under stress, are frequently known to be bad at distinguishing between facts and interpretations or between specific descriptions (e.g., "The ratio of supervision to employees is 1 to 21); and judgments ("There is inadequate supervision"). Worse still, experts often mix facts, interpretations, and advice-giving in their *technical* reports.

    All of the above deficiencies tend to inflame the hearer, increase the conflict, give primacy to emotionality over rationality, and inhibit productive work.

4. **Consequence Management**

    Because most groups do not track follow-through of agreements made at meetings, are not well sponsored, have no single-point accountability, and do not have clear outcome expectations, they are not equipped either to reward or reprimand effective and ineffective work. Absence, tardiness, sending substitutes, and not following through become normative.

The above are only some of the key elements of task force meetings that must be addressed for effective work to occur. In gathering data in these areas, it is apparent that when these elements are absent from a task force, they are also likely to be absent in the organization.[39] Sponsorship may be vague. Facilitation probably belongs to those in power, because, in that organization competency probably is not a major criteria for advancement or leadership. Technical information is likely to be shared poorly or shared in a climate of hassle rather than understanding. Any consequence management may be but a fantasy. Turning these factors around in task forces and committees can be a strong intervention in the organization if the top sponsor is ready to support such change. Far too much training in meeting effectiveness, however, misses the dimensions listed here. Because most organizations have a multitude of ad hoc groups, project teams, committees, and/or task forces, the opportunity to impact organizations with an effective strategy in this area is immense.

---

[39] *Task Force Performance Profile.*

Appendix Q

The OD (Organizational Development) Practitioner as Organizer

Proactive Consulting

Walking the Empowerment Tightrope . . . *is written for a manager/supervisor. This paper, written for consultants, describes a* proactive consultant style *that could support the manager's effort. This piece is critical of consultants who take a passive role. We would be equally critical of consultants who try to take over. I think this approach is balanced between those two extremes.*

Some 20 years ago I attended a conference of OD practitioners where our value orientation was measured. About 85% of the attendees scored as sociocentrics, that is, as people whose values were organized by process rather than ends values. These participants favored consensual governance as the primary decision-making style. The leaders chose a directive style compatible with only 5% of the participants, purposely to stimulate the contrast.

I scored with the 5%. Of course I enjoyed the conference because it was being led in a style compatible to my own. I was intrigued that many sociocentric participants struggled and indeed got quite angry with these dictatorial leaders. The sociocentric is likely to lead with the question, "Who decided?" while the ends-oriented attendee would lead with, "What was decided?" Means versus ends . . . an old tension. Of course this is not an either/or issue. Finding a balance is critical.

The following is a case for the directive side of OD work, which I think is poorly represented in practice and literature. The OD practice seems to attract people who prefer less directive behaviors, such as data gathering, process observation, or team building on call rather than as part of a strategic plan. More proactive behaviors such as advocacy, strategizing, or active facilitation of problem-solving processes have not been as widespread.

There are many excellent reasons why OD has been influenced by socio-centric values. The early 20th century world into which our profession was born was dominated by authoritarian business structures. The industrial scene at the beginning of the 20th century had many character-istics of a serf culture. Our institutions needed a strong sociocentric emphasis. Labor unions advocated for the downtrodden. New under-standings of group dynamics and democratic management processes were a welcome relief. However, such processes still remain functionally unknown to most managers despite abundant popular articles and research supporting democracy in the work place. So, sociocentric values continually need to be affirmed if there is to be productivity, quality, safety, and high morale. However, the beginning OD practitioner is often driven to an extreme sociocentric stance because of a lack of experience, confidence, and clarity.

The OD practitioners' lead questions must of necessity be, "What are your needs?" and "What do you want?" Not bad questions if they are ready to listen, suggest, advocate, educate, apply standards, and be forth-right with opinions about what works and what does *not* work in strate-gic methodologies.

The nondirective tilt of most practitioners has contributed to a percep-tion of OD as primarily a responsive function. Such OD consultants help this or that group with people problems. OD therefore often is identified with human resource or personnel, which are driven by personnel poli-cies and procedures and are intended as policy and people-support func-tions. However, in this "organizer" model *OD is driven by the organiza-tional mission, values, and business objectives, and supports strategies to achieve these.* For me the OD function is better located with the business unit than with Human Resources. Even better is for OD to be its own function reporting to the CEO.

With such an organizational location, the OD practitioner is well posi-tioned to be an "organizer,"[40] a term borrowed from community action. "Put your skin in the game"[41] is the motto. This means that the organizer will take risks and will be held accountable like everyone else for achieving the business objectives of the client. There are big stakes in organizations.

People are living out their lives there. The stance of the organizer is that he/she is a player in an important game. However, the analogy breaks down if the organizer is seen as partial to any one group: e.g., union, hourlies, mid- or top management. This organizer helps the whole organization achieve its goals.

About 10 years ago Ron Short suggested a *paradigm shift* for the practice of OD.[42] He contrasted nine categories. I mention only two here. The implication of these shifts can significantly alter a consultant's practice.

Our Current Organizing Myth	**A Paradigm Shift**
Change is brought about by the collaborative communications between skilled, well-informed people.	*Change* is a nonrational process. Change is brought about by transformation of the context, not by incremental change.
The *consultant* therefore is an educator, data collector, feedback mechanism, and facilitator of process.	The *consultant* is an active agent of change; directive, charged with changing structure, not primarily concerned with how well people are communicating.

I am grateful to Ron for this leap in thinking. It was indeed a paradigm shift for me as well as a model for the more directive side of OD. For me the word *organizer* has helped make further sense of his paradigm.

---

[40] Thanks to Rob Schachter for this analogy and dialogue about this concept.

[41] Ibid.

[42] Structural Family Therapy and Consultative Practice: A Paradigm Shift for Organizational Development. *Consultation: An International Journal,* Vol. 4 No. 2, pp. 99-118.

To function effectively within an organization, organizers must be aligned with the sponsor. To reach that alignment they will do the following:

- Seek clarity about the real (not slogan) mission, values, and business objectives.

- Help build strategies to achieve the business objectives.

- Help create alignment with those strategies.

- Encourage the development of financial and nonfinancial indicators.

- Include in the strategy the sharing of appropriate information (e.g., monthly status of indicators) with all employees.

- Consult within the context of these strategies, business objectives, and indicators while continually supporting the re-examination of all of these in order to keep current with changing circumstances.

- Challenge misalignment; aid and abet the communication of emerging problems.

- Encourage problem solving with the appropriate employees when indicators are lower than intended and encourage celebrations when they are on target.

- Coach the boss about how to be the type of sponsor who gives solid backing through supportive words, resource allocation, prioritized tasks, monitored activities, clear directives to the subjects of change, and consequence management.

- Constantly look for dysfunctional patterns[43] and actively help to shift those patterns.

- Stay clear that the OD practitioner does *not* have line authority but is an agent of change.

---

[43] Such as illustrated in Chapter 4 and in the Action Idea for Factor 25.

Again, all of the above is done in concert with the sponsoring boss with whom there is continuous dialogue. The organizer never loses sight of the need for balance between the immediate daily tasks of the organization that must be achieved and the long-term building of a more effective organization to achieve better the values and business objectives. This includes identifying and training a cadre of employees and managers for change agent roles.

Also, the organizer works with all segments of the organization. This work is done in the halls, lunch rooms, and meetings of the organization. The old paradigm OD practitioner may sit through a meeting that is failing and later give feedback about the process. Imagine a sponsor saying, "Don't tell me the meeting failed and you were there. Why didn't you do something?" The new paradigm organizer will act during the meeting to help it succeed. A sponsor with whom I worked made it clear to me and to his other employees that if a meeting was not working, he expected all of us to stand up and say, "Time out," if we must, and then help the group get on track. The organizer educates the sponsor to authorize the organizer and all attendees to create success proactively in all organizational endeavors. In essence, do not just sit there; create the outcome.

Also, when the organizer shares the values and business directions, then he/she will not let observations of poor mid-management, sponsorship, or shoddy quality go unnoticed. While an organizer will first encourage and coach others to report and/or apply problem-solving efforts to any practice that does not support the values and business objectives, he/she is not willing to walk away and have nothing happen. The organizer will not let the sponsor/boss be blindsided by information that is important to the success of the operation, which is known to the organizer and which others are choosing to hide.

This organizer will never be satisfied working with any group without reference to a larger strategy. He/she works continually for organizational alignment and takes risks to get painful information shared. He/she actively engages in dialogues in order to achieve maximum alignment with the sponsor. When that happens, power is unleashed. Of course, excesses will happen and the organizer will sometimes overfunction. Just as the nondirective-oriented practitioner will be too passive at times, the organizer will be inappropriately active at times. This activity includes the offering of both solicited and unsolicited opinions about methodologies. Presumably, the organizer has expert knowledge about critical issues that make or break change projects.

For example, distinctions between influence and decision making are fuzzy in most organizations. With true clarity that the boss (who has hired the organizer) is the decision maker, the two then can fully engage in dialogue with the organizer, freely offering opinions. The organizer is an agent of change with power derived from the degree to which he/she is aligned with the key line-manager. This alignment is only effectively achieved through dialogue. If an organizer does not believe in the decisions being made about goals, values, and implementation strategies, then he/she should make this clear and get out of the way.

If one believes in the direction, then the organizer will be ready to put her/his "skin in the game," functioning in the organization as a community organizer may function in a community. This demands that the organizer behave in the following ways:

- Never play "boss." When confronted with *undo* resistance, the standard response is: "There must be some mistake. This is not my 'program,' even though I certainly support it. Perhaps you need (further?) conversations with your boss about his/her intentions and the role I'm to play with you."

- Hear resistance, disbelief, cynicism in an empathic way and sharply distinguish it from your own experience. For example, if workers mistrust the sponsoring boss whom the practitioner trusts, the organizer is able to say, "I get it. Your trust in (the boss) is very low. I have had a different experience. If I didn't trust (the boss), I wouldn't be here. I value your experience and I also value mine. You may see me as naive and say that I have not known this boss as long as you have, but I have to trust my own experience *and* pay a lot of attention to yours. However, I am not here to quarrel with your experience with the boss. I am here to help you and the boss reach specific agreements with each other toward a more productive working relationship."

- Provide eyes and ears to the boss. The organizer must strategize to help others give opinions, feelings, and facts *directly* to the boss. But when something is being *withheld* that affects the success of the change activity, that is, when others will not come forth with critical data, the organizer must bite the bullet and find effective ways to share that with the boss. The ethics for the organizer with "skin in the game" is to make sure that information is available and to trust the boss to use that withheld information wisely. If such trust and subsequent confirmation of the trust do *not* exist, the consultant must confront this with the boss.

- Constantly strategize with others and act to achieve the goals. This may mean enabling employees who are advocating change but have no line management support to be heard. It may mean questioning the skills, knowledge, or willingness to change observed in lower level managers or employees, or confronting the sponsor. The differentiation here is to remember where the sponsorship *and* the actual implementation is and not get seduced into being a savior, urging others on despite all odds when either sponsorship or implementation by employees is dragging.

All of the above is done in the context of continual dialogue with all levels of the organization. The organizer moves across the continuum of consultant behaviors doing "whatever it takes" to support alignment and to assist the organization to achieve its objectives. This alignment creates a delicate balancing act. The organizer may be accused of being too close to the boss and being partial. He/she may be accused of favoring the workers. The organizer will walk that tightrope and occasionally fall off. *That* is when the organizer will realize his/her "skin *is* in the game."

Appendix R

Graphic Illustration of the Change Process

Original System

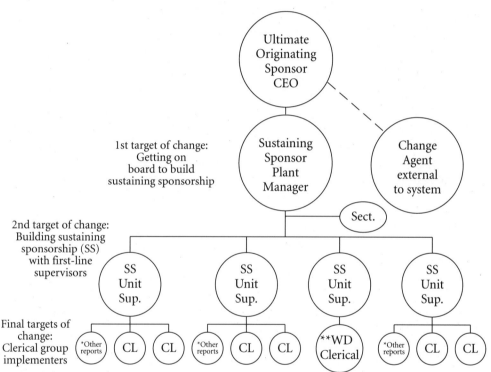

The initial decision to make the change belonged to the CEO. The clerical staff and supervisors had high influence about the logistics of the work-redesign implementation. The decision to accept the implementation recommendations (primarily developed by the clerical group) was delegated by the vice president to the plant manager, with the understanding that clerical resources *were* to be pooled.

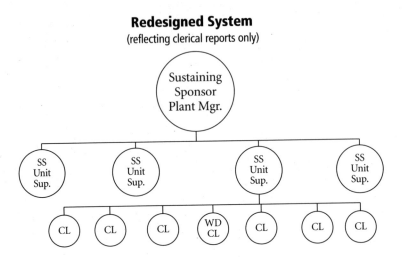

Redesigned System

(reflecting clerical reports only)

Notice that in the redesigned system, single-point accountability was allocated to one unit supervisor who, in turn, had a work director with single-point. (See the Action Idea for Factor 22).